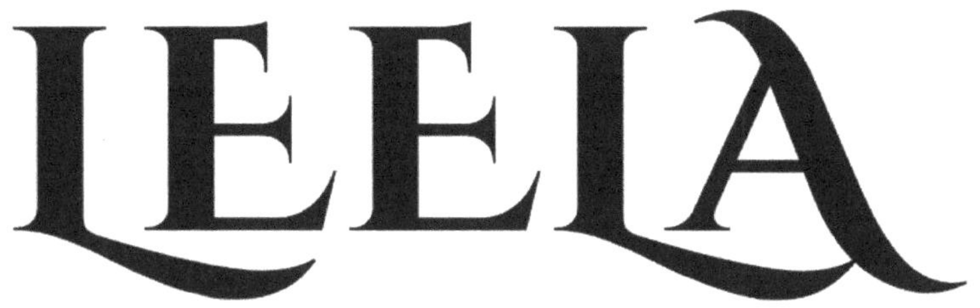

अयं संसारः एकः मञ्चः अस्ति तथा च वयं सर्वे भिन्नाः भिन्नाः
चरित्रभूमिकाः निर्वहन्तः स्मः

Instant Publication
Gautam Buddha Nagar
Noida - 201301
Uttar Pradesh, India
Email I'd: instantpublication.org@gmail.com

"Leela"
By: - Mukul Phate
ISBN: 978-81-19422-79-1
Non-Fiction 1st Edition 2024
Publisher: - Instant Publication
Typesetting: - Puja Kumari
Cover Designing: - Mukul Phate
Price: - INR 799

RESPECT FOR ACTING

Acknowledging the craft alone is not enough to show respect for acting; one must also recognize the depth of talent, vulnerability, and commitment that actors bring to their roles. Acting is a complex art form that calls for emotional intelligence, sensitivity, and a deep comprehension of human behaviour. It is not only about acting.

Acting is fundamentally about telling the truth. In order to depict characters as accurately as possible, actors delve into the minds of their subjects to reveal desires, anxieties, and motivations. This calls for a profound degree of reflection and self-awareness because actors frequently use their personal experiences to bring their characters to life. Recognizing the bravery required to expose weaknesses for the purpose of storytelling on stage or in front of the camera is a necessary component of respect for acting.

A strong work ethic is necessary for acting. In order to perfect their craft, actors study a wide range of methods, dialects, and movement styles. They put in endless hours practicing, learning lines by heart, and carefully and nuancedly assuming the roles they play. Respecting acting is appreciating the self-control and tenacity needed to succeed in such a cutthroat and demanding industry.

Being an actor is a team sport. In order to trust the directors and other actors in the cast, actors must give up their egos in favour of the group's vision for the play. Honouring the contributions of each person involved in the creative process from the playwright who develops the script to the crew members who work behind the scenes to make it come to life is essential to respecting performing.

In addition, acting fulfils an essential social purpose. Actors have the ability to inspire change, arouse empathy, and provoke thought via storytelling. They give voice to underrepresented viewpoints, challenge social norms, and face hard truths. Respecting acting entails acknowledging its influence on culture and promoting discourse on significant topics.

Acting requires adaptability and determination. Actors must face industry rejection, criticism and unpredictability with grace and determination. They must be willing to take risks, step out of their comfort zone and embrace failure as an opportunity to grow. To respect acting is to respect the determination and determination of those who pursue it as a career.

In summary, respect for acting includes an awareness of the creativity, commitment, and societal influence of the discipline in addition to enthusiasm for individual performances. Actors are storytellers, truth-seekers, and change-agents in addition to being entertainers. By recognizing the intricacy and importance of their work, we pay tribute to the performers' priceless contribution to the field of culture.

INTRODUCTION

"Embracing Leela: Infusing Acting with Divine Playfulness and Authenticity"

In acting, "Leela" represents a deep idea derived from Indian traditional performing arts, especially theatre and dance. It symbolizes the essence of unplanned delight and creativity, the heavenly play, and the artistic manifestation of gods and goddesses. In the realm of acting, being aware of and embracing the Leela notion can greatly enhance performances by giving them a feeling of divine fun, genuineness, and vibrancy.

Fundamentally, Leela explores the philosophical and spiritual aspects of human expression in addition to performing arts. It is the cosmic drama playing out through the medium of life itself, the dance of existence. We must examine its beginnings, its expressions in other artistic traditions, and its practical application in the acting craft in order to fully understand its relevance.

The origins of the term "Leela" can be traced back to Indian mythology and philosophy. It alludes to Hinduism's their dramas, or the divine play of the gods and goddesses. These heavenly plays are symbolic depictions of cosmic laws, spiritual truths, and the never-ending dance of creation, preservation, and destruction rather than just entertaining plays.

Leela is a major motif in Indian classical dance styles including Bharatanatyam, Kathak, and Odyssey. Dancers represent gods such as Krishna, Shiva, and Devi, expressing the divine attributes they represent and depicting their legendary adventures. Dancers embody Leela through complex body language, gestures, and expressions, bringing the holy force into their performances.

Leela serves as a guiding principle in Indian classical theatre, sometimes referred to as Natya. Performers adopt personas from Hindu epics such as the Mahabharata and the Ramayana, representing gods, devils, heroes, and heroines. Their performances take the audience into the world of myth and legend and invoke the divine, making them more than just representations.

The notion of Leela is not limited to Indian traditional arts; it finds resonance among actors across the globe. Shakespeare and other writers who delved into themes of fate, destiny, and the relationship between men and gods are credited with popularizing the concept of the "divine play" in Western theatre. Figures such as Puck from "A Midsummer Night's Dream" personify the playful antics of supernatural beings and represent the mischievous spirit of Leela.

The idea of Leela is consistent with modern theories of acting, like the emphasis on spontaneity and honesty by Sanford Meisner and the concept of "the magic if" by Konstantin Stanislavski. Stanislavski believed that performers should playfully explore the possibilities by putting themselves in the shoes of their characters. Meisner, on the other hand, believes that the performance should develop naturally when players act authentically in response to their instincts and the actions of their scene partners.

Practically speaking, integrating Leela into acting entails a few essential components:

1. **Spontaneity**: Performers work to be spontaneous so that their shows can develop naturally on the spot. They welcome the unexpected and keep an open mind to any creative ideas that come to them when they rehearse and perform.

2. **Joyfulness**: Performers embrace the creative process as a source of inspiration and fulfilment, and they approach their work with a sense of joy and enthusiasm. They enjoy delving deeply into the human experience and assuming the roles of their characters.

3. **Playfulness**: Actors experiment with many choices and approaches to their characters, bringing a mood of playfulness to their performances. They continue to approach every practice and performance as a light-hearted investigation of possibilities, maintaining a spirit of inquiry and discovery.

4. **Connection**: To create genuine and captivating performances, actors aim to build a strong bond with their characters by referencing their own feelings and experiences.

They make an effort to capture the spirit of the characters they represent, letting their inner selves come through.

5. Presence: By firmly establishing themselves in the present and giving their all to their roles and the play's universe, actors develop a strong sense of presence. They sustain a high level of awareness and involvement by staying vigilant and sensitive to their environment.

Actors can imbue their performances with the essence of Leela by adhering to these rules, turning their work into a holy sacrifice and allowing spectators to witness the heavenly play being performed. Leela reminds us, whether on stage or film, of the timeless dance of creation at the core of all artistic expression and the transcendent power of storytelling.

TRIBUTE TO WORLD'S BEST ACTOR

BAHIRJEE NAIK

[Third Eye of Chhatrapati Shivaji Maharaj]

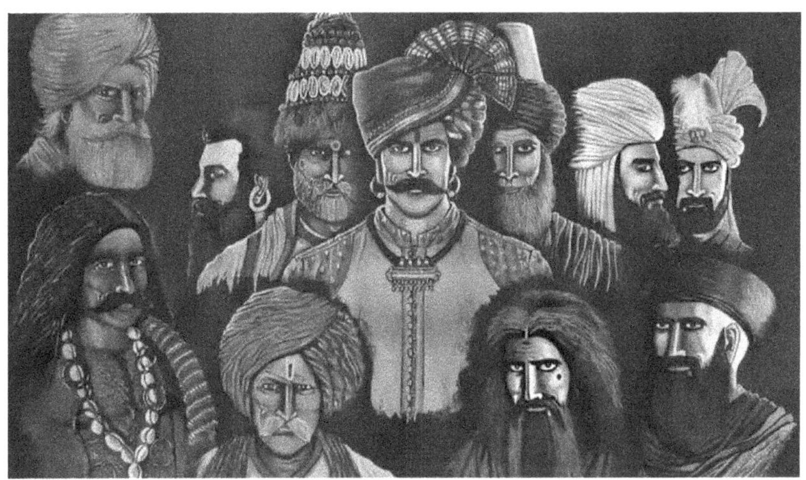

According to me, Bahirjee Naik, Unknown legend but the top actor in the world and praised as the top spy for Chhatrapati Shivaji Maharaj. He was not just good on in war tactics could also copy animal sounds, a key trick for secret spy work. Known as the "third eye" of the Maratha Ruler Chhatrapati Shivaji Maharaj, Bahirjee Naik was key in getting info and helping the Maratha empire stay safe and win. His many skills and true heart make him a key part of Maratha tales.

INDEX

10.3 Recognizing and accommodating various directing philosophies

11. Ethics and Responsibility

11.1 Actors have an obligation to represent a range of viewpoints and cultures

11.2 Ethical issues in depicting delicate or contentious characters or subjects

11.3 Juggling creative liberty with social

12. Artistic Reflections

● Stage of Souls: A Journey Through the Actor's Life (poem on actors)

13. Inspiration from the Greats

● Examples of the Best Actors with Their Bios

1.UNDERSTANDING ACTING

1.1 What is Acting?

The complex art form of acting entails taking on the persona of a character and convincingly presenting their motivations, feelings, and experiences to a viewer. Bringing stories to life on stage, in movies, on television, or in other media is the fundamental goal of acting. It calls for a blend of aptitude, expertise, commitment, and originality. Acting is fundamentally the art of pretending. Actors adopt personas, putting aside their own identities to inhabit those of fictional or real-life characters. Through this technique, the actor can portray the character more realistically by developing a deep understanding of the character's motivations, personality, and background.

Emotional expression is one of acting's core abilities. A vast spectrum of emotions, from happiness and love to rage and grief, must be tapped into by actors in order to effectively portray them to the audience. Because of the characters' depth of emotion, the audience is able to relate to them and get emotionally involved in their journey. Acting requires not just emotional expression but also physicality.

Movement, gestures, and body language can convey just as much information as words, if not more. To portray the physicality of their characters and improve the narrative, actors need to be skilled with their bodies. Acting also requires vocal expression, which is another essential component. The tone, pitch, rhythm, and accent of an actor's speech can have a big impact on how the audience perceives a character. By developing their vocal skills, performers can add complexity and nuance to their performances, which increases the overall effect on the audience.

A great deal of imagination and inventiveness are also necessary for acting. Performers need to be able to enter made-up environments, communicate with ethereal characters, and react to scenarios they have created. Acting is a fascinating art form because it requires the ability to suspend disbelief and totally immerse oneself in the fictional environment. Furthermore, acting is a cooperative activity that necessitates communication and coordination. To make a production come to life, actors must collaborate closely with directors, other cast members, and staff members. In addition to ensuring that all parties are working toward the same goal, effective collaboration contributes to the creation of a coherent and appealing end result.

In conclusion, acting is a sophisticated and varied art form that calls for physicality, vocal technique, inventiveness, teamwork, and emotional expression. It enables performers to inhabit characters, bring tales to life, and establish a strong emotional connection with viewers. Acting is a timeless and vital form of artistic expression because it has the ability to inspire, amuse, and stimulate thought whether it is performed on stage or screen.

1.2 Main Types of Acting

There are many different approaches and styles within acting, each having unique methods and traits. Here are some of the main types of acting:

1. **Method Acting**: Method acting, which was pioneered by professionals like Constantin Stanislavski and made famous by stars like Marlon Brando and Robert De Niro, places a strong emphasis on psychological reality and emotional sincerity. In order to establish a strong emotional connection with their characters, actors who employ this technique frequently draw from their own life experiences and feelings.

2. **Classical Acting**: Classical acting is rooted in the traditions of Shakespearean drama and ancient Greek theatre. It emphasizes stylized movement, elevated language, and strict devotion to performing practices. Actors that work in this genre frequently receive intense instruction in verse speaking, diction, and voice projection.

3. **Physical Theatre**: Without mainly depending on spoken words, physical theatre uses dance, mime, and movement to convey message and emotion. In physical theatre, actors express themselves primarily via their bodies, using methods including group choreography, mask work, and gesture storytelling.

4. **Improvisational Acting**: Improvisational acting, or improv, involves performing without a script or predetermined dialogue. Actors rely on spontaneity, quick thinking, and collaboration to create scenes, characters, and narratives in

real-time. Improv exercises are often used in actor training to develop creativity, flexibility, and ensemble skills.

5. **Meisner Technique**: This acting technique, created by Sanford Meisner, places an emphasis on actors' genuine, in-the-moment emotions. Meisner Technique techniques, such emotional preparation and repetition, assist actors in developing responsiveness, emotional honesty, and authenticity in their performances.

6. **Comedic Acting**: Comedy calls for a unique set of abilities, such as timing, physicality, and precise line delivery. To make the audience laugh, comedic actors frequently use exaggerated facial expressions, funny timing, and voice inflections.

7. **Voice Acting**: Voice acting is acting without using one's body; instead, character, emotion, and story are communicated entirely through voice acting. Voice actors use their voices to bring characters to life in a variety of roles and locations in a variety of media, such as radio dramas, video games, animation, and audiobooks.

These are but a handful of the several forms of acting that are out there, each with its own special difficulties, methods, and creative prospects. The demands of a given role or production may force actors to specialize in one style or blend aspects from numerous techniques into their performances.

1.3 Definitions of Theatre Drama and Film Acting

Theatre Drama –

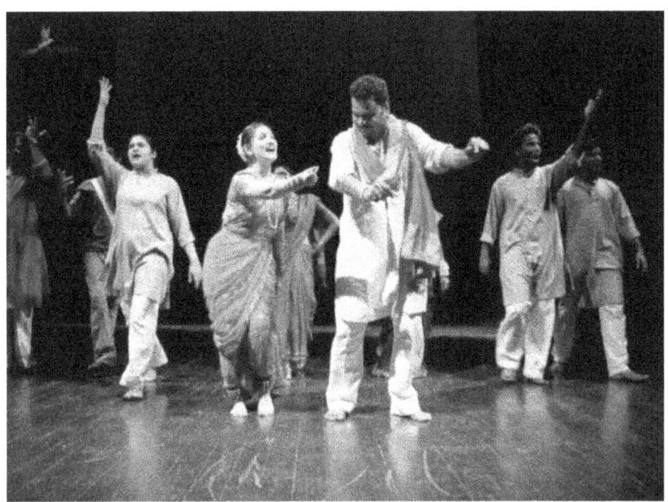

Acting for theatre play involves a complex fusion of abilities, feelings, and methods to bring characters to life on stage. Fundamentally, it's the skill of convincingly and credible expressing a character's intentions, ideas, and feelings. It involves comprehending the psychology of the characters, the relationships between them, and the environments they live in. Let's examine the many facets that go into the art of theatrical drama acting in more detail.

A great actor must, first and foremost, have a thorough comprehension of the script. To understand the subtleties of the character's journey, their arc, and the topics discussed in the play, they carefully study the text. Examining the character's past, present, goals, conflicts, and interactions with other characters are all part of this process. Performers are able to portray their characters more realistically when they fully immerse themselves in the play's setting.

The capacity to relate to the characters on stage is one of the core elements of theatre drama acting. In order to bring their performances to life, actors need to put themselves in the shoes of their characters and draw from their own feelings and experiences. In order to portray the inner workings of their characters' minds, actors must possess a high level of emotional intelligence and vulnerability, as they must delve into the depths of human emotion.

When it comes to performing in theatre drama, physicality counts. Actors engage with the audience, portray emotions, and transmit subtext with their bodies. Every physical detail, including posture, movement, and facial expressions and gestures, is skilfully designed to complement the character's portrayal and communicate their emotional condition. An actor with skill may express meaning through body language alone, saying volumes without saying a word.

Another key component of theatre drama acting is voice modulation. To effectively communicate the words and emotions of their characters to the audience, actors need to have a strong command of voice projection, articulation, and intonation. Whether they're shouting out an impassioned monologue or making an intimate confession, actors utilize their voices as potent tools to enthral and involve audiences.

The technical parts of acting are important, but actors also need to develop a strong sense of presence and camaraderie with other performers. Since acting is a collaborative art form, the dynamic interactions between actors on stage are essential to the success of performances. This calls for spontaneity, attentive listening, and the capacity to honestly react to the deeds and responses of other characters.

In addition, stage drama acting calls for a deep comprehension of blocking, staging, and spatial awareness. Actors have to move precisely over the physical space of the stage so that their actions support the narrative and keep the audience's attention. To achieve a smooth and engrossing theatrical performance, this entails practicing and perfecting every scene.

Another characteristic of theatre drama acting is embracing the unpredictable nature of live performance. Theatre performers have to give their best performances in-person, with little room for error, unlike actors in films or television shows where sequences can be edited and retakes are allowed. This necessitates perseverance, flexibility, and a readiness to welcome the unplanned in the face of unforeseen obstacles.

Furthermore, acting in theatre dramas demands a strong dedication to the profession and an unwavering pursuit of greatness. To develop one's abilities and craft, it takes endless hours of practice, experimenting, and introspection. To advance as performers, actors must continuously step outside of their comfort zones, take calculated chances, and experiment with novel approaches.

In the end, dramatic theatre acting is a transformative art form that profoundly moves, inspires, and provokes audiences. It encourages audiences to share in the victories, tribulations, and epiphanies of the characters on stage as it honours the human experience in all its complexity. Theatre survives as a vital and important storytelling medium that cuts across time and geography because to the commitment and skill of gifted performers.

Film Acting –

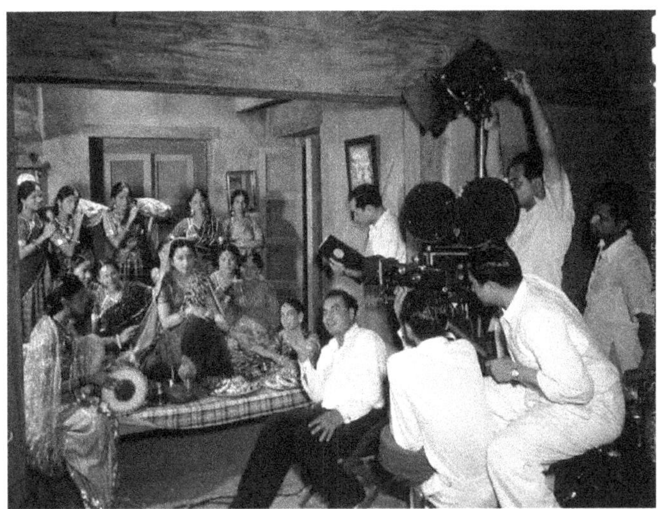

The engaging and diverse art form of film acting is responsible for bringing stories to life on screen. Film acting presents a different kind of difficulty than theatre, where performances take place in real time in front of an audience, with the goal of immortalizing moments on celluloid that viewers can relive over and over. Film actors need to be skilled in a wide range of approaches to portray the feelings, motivations, and innermost thoughts of their characters, whether it is through intimate close-ups or expansive panoramic shots. Let's examine the diverse range of abilities and subtleties that make up the film acting profession.

The capacity to communicate authenticity and emotional depth through nuanced movements and nuances is at the core of cinema acting. A more genuine approach is necessary for film acting than for theatre, where big expressions and dramatic gestures are frequently employed. In this medium, even the smallest shift in expression can convey a lot. Actors must expose their souls to the camera, giving viewers a peek into the inner thoughts of their characters, which necessitates a high degree of awareness and vulnerability.

The use of the camera as a storytelling device is one of the biggest distinctions between performing for the stage and film. In a movie, the camera is the viewer's window into the story's universe, capturing every subtlety of the performer's performance in breath-taking detail. To have their performances resonate with viewers on screen, performers in films must learn to modulate their performances to fit the needs of the camera. This includes modifying their gestures, facial emotions, and vocal delivery.

A trademark of film acting are close-ups, in particular, which let viewers notice even the most subtle emotions expressed on an actor's face. Actors have to be extremely precise and in control in order to portray complicated emotions with just a glance or a small quiver of the lip. Film performers have to be very aware of their facial expressions because the camera accentuates every little detail. This will help them look real and captivating in every scene.

Film performers need to have a strong grasp of visual storytelling in addition to the technical components of performing on screen. In contrast to theatre, where viewers' attention is fixed on the stage, film makes greater use of perspective and space. Actors need to be aware of where they are in relation to other components of the scene, such as the lighting, set, and props, as well as where they are in the frame. Their performances get depth and complexity from this level of spatial awareness, which enhances the audience's overall visual experience.

In addition, film acting frequently entails tight collaboration with directors and cinematographers to attain the intended emotional and artistic impact. Cooperation is essential, as performers need to be receptive to criticism and eager to try out various approaches to their roles. Actors are able to push the boundaries of their trade and explore new depths in their performances because to this collaborative approach that encourages originality and innovation.

The capacity to change to fit the needs of different genres and styles is another crucial component of being an actor in movies. Film performers need to be versatile and adaptive, able to embody a wide range of characters and settings with ease, from fast-paced action sequences to quiet, introspective tragedies. This adaptability also applies to the technical elements of performance, as performers may need to acquire new physical abilities, dialects, or accents in order to fully in hat their roles.

Film acting requires a keen understanding of pacing and rhythm, as scenes are often shot out of sequence and edited together in post-production. Actors must maintain consistency in their performances, ensuring that their character's emotional journey remains coherent and engaging throughout the film. This requires careful attention to detail and a strong sense of continuity, as actors must recreate the same emotional beats and character dynamics across multiple takes and setups.

Since sequences are frequently shot out of order and combined in post-production, cinema acting calls for a strong sense of rhythm and timing. throughout order to make their character's emotional journey throughout the movie understandable and interesting, actors need to be consistent in their portrayals. Because performers have to replicate the same emotional beats and character dynamics throughout numerous takes and setups, this calls for meticulous attention to detail and a strong sense of continuity.

1.4 Difference between Theatre Drama & Film Acting

Both cinema acting and theatre drama are performing arts that entail bringing people to life through emotive portrayal, yet they differ greatly in terms of audience experience, execution, and strategies. The main differences between cinema acting and stage drama are broken down as follows:

1. Recorded versus Live Performance:

- **Theatre Drama Acting**: Live performances take place in front of live audiences in theatres. Errors cannot be cut out of an actor's performance; they must communicate their voices and feelings to the entire audience.

- **Film Acting:** In film acting performances are recorded, photographed, and edited in post-production. Scenes are shot out of order, and actors are afforded the luxury of many takes to enhance their performances.

2. Scale of Performance:

- **Theatre Drama Acting**: Even in the rear rows of the theatre, performances in the theatre frequently call for more expressive gestures and facial expressions to communicate emotions and actions to the audience.

- **Film Acting**: Because the camera picks up on even the slightest details in body language and facial emotions, film acting is typically more nuanced and lifelike. Actors are skilled at expressing emotions with small gestures and facial expressions.

3. Audience Engagement:

- **Theatre Drama Acting**: Theatre performers engage directly with the live audience. Their ability to sense the reactions of the audience allows them to modify their performances in real time, giving them a distinct energy.

- **Film Acting**: During the filming process, actors do not engage directly with the audience. The camera lens acts as a medium for their performances, and audience reactions are seen afterwards during screenings.

4. Rehearsal Process:

- **Theatre Drama Acting**: Theatre rehearsals are long and usually focus on character development, ensemble work, and blocking, or organizing movement on stage. Live rehearsals provide actors with the chance to hone their performances.

- **Film Acting**: Rehearsals for a film are often brief, with an emphasis on technical elements like camera blocking, pacing, and acting consistency. It is possible that actors will have less time before filming to fully develop their roles.

5. Technical Considerations:

- **Theatre Drama Acting**: Without the use of microphones, theatre performers must project their voices in order for the audience to hear them. They must also be aware of visual obstructions and stage lights.

- **Film Acting**: To make sure their performances are adequately captured on camera; film actors collaborate closely with directors of photography and cinematographers. They might have to modify their performances to account for variations in lighting and camera angles.

6. Performance Style:

- **Theatre Drama Acting**: Dramatic theatre acting frequently highlights larger-than-life performances appropriate for the theatre environment. To communicate the objectives of their characters, actors sometimes use exaggerated emotions and body language.

- **Film Acting**: With a focus on nuanced facial expressions and inner feelings, film acting is typically more grounded and intimate. Actors use subtle performances that ring true on film to communicate depth.

In conclusion, while bringing characters to life is a common goal of both theatre drama and film acting, there are certain differences between the two in terms of performance scale, audience involvement, rehearsal method, technical considerations, and performance style. Throughout their careers, many performers find joy in experimenting with both types of acting since they each present different difficulties and opportunities.

2. Let's explore the multifaceted qualities and traits that audiences seek in their cinematic performers

When viewers get comfortable in their seats, they start a trip filled with emotion, imagination, and storytelling. The actors who give characters life on screen are at the centre of this cinematic experience. Actors have the ability to enthral audiences and make an enduring impact, whether they are playing lovers, friends, villains, or heroes. However, when seeing a movie, what qualities do viewers specifically look for in an actor? Let's examine the various characteristics and attributes that viewers look for in their actors in motion pictures.

● **Authenticity**: More than anything else, viewers want sincerity in the acts they see. individuals want to feel as though they are interacting with real individuals who have genuine feelings, experiences, and motives when they watch characters on screen. Actors must completely enter their roles in order to be authentic, bringing authenticity, honesty, and vulnerability to their performances. The genuineness of a character's journey can captivate spectators, causing them to get emotionally engrossed in the story as it is being told.

● **Emotional Range**: Viewers want to see actors who can portray a wide range of emotions on screen, as the human experience is a tapestry of feelings. Viewers seek out performances that elicit a visceral response and resonate on an emotional level, ranging from joy and laughter to grief and rage. Performers who are adept at evoking a wide range of emotions with delicacy, depth, and sensitivity immerse viewers in the action, letting them experience the ups and downs as well as the victories and transformations of the characters.

● **Versatility**: When performers exhibit variety and range, they can move between roles and genres with ease, which is something that audiences find appealing. Whether playing a humorous role in a light-hearted romantic comedy or exploring deep drama in a moving independent film, versatile actors demonstrate their versatility and competence by embodying a range of roles with sincerity and conviction. Actors that possess versatility are able to take on a range of roles, which pushes their personal boundaries and keeps spectators surprised and delighted.

● **Chemistry**: Many iconic movies revolve around the dynamic relationships between characters, and viewers are drawn to performers who can genuinely capture chemistry on screen. The chemistry between performers enhances the depth, authenticity, and emotional resonance of the storytelling experience, whether it is through the soft intimacy between lovers, the unbreakable tie of friendship, or the crackling tension between enemies. The actors' tangible connection and electrifying energy attract audiences, giving the connections on screen a vibrant, captivating, and unforgettable quality.

● **Depth**: Any movie's characters are its heart and soul, and viewers are drawn to performers who can give these fictitious characters nuance, complexity, and humanity. Understanding character motivations, internal conflicts, and personal growth arcs is the key to delivering a performance with depth. Viewers value performers who have the ability to show a character's innermost thoughts, frailties, and vulnerabilities by removing layers of the character's psychology. Depth enables performers to provide richness, genuineness, and emotional resonance to their roles, allowing viewers to identify with the hardships and victories of the characters.

● **Presence**: An actor's performance can be enhanced and audiences captivated from the first moment they step on screen by having a powerful screen presence. Actors that possess charisma, confidence, or magnetism, or both, command attention and make an effect on the audience that doesn't go away. Actors that possess presence command the screen with strength, composure, and gravitas through their body language, facial expressions, and voice delivery. Presence incorporates both physicality and emotional intensity. Audiences are compelled to become involved with the characters and their tales by a strong presence that immerses them in the movie's world.

● **Physicality**: When it comes to on-screen actions, emotions, and character attributes, physicality is essential. Actors use their bodies as expressive instruments to give their characters life, from subtle movements and facial reactions to dynamic movement and physical transformations. Whether through elegant choreography, dramatic combat scenes, or immersive physical transformations, actors who can harness the power of physicality to create memorable and impactful performances are highly appreciated by audiences. Physicality enhances a performance's depth, realism, and visual appeal while also providing audiences with a more satisfying cinematic experience.

● **Subtlety**: Audiences seek subtlety and nuance in acting just as much as emotional intensity. With subtle facial expressions, subtle body language, and subtle vocal inflections, performers can portray a wide range of complicated emotions and internal conflicts. Subtle actors captivate viewers with their quiet passion instead of resorting to melodrama or exaggerated performances, giving them the opportunity to understand the richness and depth of a character's inner world. Through the addition of layers of depth and authenticity, subtlety encourages audiences to interact with the intricacies and nuances of the storytelling experience.

● **Believability**: Fundamentally, acting is about evoking a sense of believable immersion that draws viewers into the movie's universe. The goal of the audience is to completely lose oneself in the narrative and characters that are being portrayed on television. For a performance to be believable, actors must embody their characters with conviction, sincerity, and meticulous attention to detail. This means that every element of a performance, from physique to dialogue delivery, must be authentic and true to the character's core. Audiences are drawn into the story and develop a strong emotional bond with the characters and their journey when performers are able to make their performances seem realistic and relevant.

● **Consistency**: To preserve a character's integrity in their portrayal throughout the movie, consistency is essential. Performers who can portray a character's goals, personality, and emotional journey consistently are appreciated by audiences. To keep viewers interested in the plot, performers should aim for continuity in their performances, whether that means keeping a constant accent, manner, or emotional state. Maintaining consistency makes it possible for viewers to become emotionally invested in the characters and their stories, which improves the viewing experience as a whole.

3. EXPLORING GENRES

3.1 Genres and Their Types

What Do Film Genres Mean?

Films are classified into genres based on their stylistic or narrative components. Characters, settings, story devices, and tone can all be influenced by a movie's genre. For instance, battle sequences and slow-motion camera shots are common in action films. Jump scares and a focus on action rather than speech are common in horror films.

Action, adventure, comedy, drama, fantasy, horror, musicals, mystery, romance, science fiction, sports, thriller, and Western are among the most common film genres. Examples of topics that can be found in action, drama, or thriller films include war and zombies.

What Is a Subgenre in Film?

A subgenre in cinema is a distinct kind of filmmaking that fits into a larger genre, such as comedy, horror, or drama. Subgenres vary in terms of style. For instance, comedies include romantic comedies and slapstick cartoons, yet there are major differences between the two in terms of plot, dialogue, aesthetics, and humour. Numerous diverse subgenres within a single cinema genre are possible, and they frequently overlap and have things in common.

1 - Action Genre

Action films are fast-paced and packed with action, including pursuit scenes, battle scenes, and slow-motion images. They may include action-packed stunts, martial arts, or superheroes. These fast-paced flicks focus more on how the plot is carried out than on the plot itself. Action films keep viewers on the edge of their seats and are fascinating to watch. The action genre includes films about cops, disasters, and some spy stories.

2 - Adventure Genre

Because the adventure and action genres are so similar, adventure films are occasionally billed as action/adventure films. Adventure films typically have many of the same fundamental features as action films, with the environment serving as the key distinction. Adventure films are frequently set in a remote, exotic, or strange location. Swashbuckler films and survival films can be categorised under this heading. The adventure subgenre is represented by the Pirates of the Caribbean film series from 2003.

3 - Comedy Genre

Comedy films are light-hearted and enjoyable. The comedy theme of these films frequently involves putting a character in a difficult, entertaining, or humorous situation that they are not equipped to handle. A good comedy film should focus less on making jokes all the time and more on telling a realistic, true story with complex characters who take away a valuable lesson. Comedy subgenres include mockumentaries, dark comedies (or black comedies), romantic comedies, parodies and spoofs, and slapstick comedies.

4 - Drama Genre

Drama stories typically have many conflicts and high stakes. They require that every character and scene advance the plot since they are plot-driven. Dramas have a definite narrative plot structure and often feature emotionally charged individuals in settings that are either extreme or taken from real life. Historical drama or costume drama, romantic drama, teen drama, medical drama, docudrama, film noir, and neo-noir are examples of films that fall within the drama sub-genre.

5 - Fantasy Genre

Fantasy films often include magical and supernatural elements that don't exist in reality. While some films mix fantasy elements with real-world settings, many of them construct wholly fictional planets complete with their own set of rules, logic, and populations of extraordinary animals and races. Fantasy films are speculative yet unrelated to truth or scientific fact, just like science fiction films. Fantasy subgenres include things like high fantasy, fairy tales, and magical realism. A classic example of a fantasy movie is the Harry Potter film series, which is based on the books by J.K. Rowling and follows a young boy at the Hogwarts School of Witchcraft and Wizardry.

6 - Horror Genre

People who watch horror films often experience components that fill them with an intense terror and dread. In order to play on viewers' anxieties or nightmares, horror films frequently feature serial killers or monsters as persistent, terrible antagonists. Horror fans deliberately seek out these films for the adrenaline rush that ghosts, gore, monsters, and jump scares provide. The macabre, ghost stories, gothic horror, science fiction horror, supernatural, dark fantasy, psychological horror, and slasher film subgenres are all examples of horror films.

7 - Music Genre

Songs or musical numbers are incorporated into musical films' narratives to advance the plot or further the character development. Although not exclusive to that genre, musicals are frequently associated with romantic flicks. Large-scale stage-like performances are a feature of musical films, and the scenes incorporate any essential premises or character components.

8 - Mystery Genre

The focus of mystery films is the enigma, which is frequently being solved by a detective or amateur sleuth. It's always tenses watching the protagonist of a mystery film as they piece together the events and investigate suspects to find the answer to the main mystery. The mystery subgenre frequently includes the two subgenres of hardboiled noirs and police procedurals.

9 - Romance Genre

The love stories in romance films. The two protagonists at their centre explore many aspects of love, such as connections, sacrifice, marriage, obsession, or destruction. In romance films, difficulties for the love characters to overcome occasionally include sickness, betrayal, tragedy, or other challenges. Popular romance subgenres include romantic comedies, gothic romance, and romantic action.

10 - Science Fiction Genre

The sci-fi genre creates imagined components not found in the real world in its planets and parallel dimensions. Science fiction covers a wide range of topics, including time travel, space travel, futuristic settings, and the effects of scientific and technical advancements. For the audience to get into the plot and universe of a science fiction film, rigorous world-building and tremendous attention to detail are typically required.

11 - Sports Genre

Sports-themed films usually focus on a team, a specific player, or a fan, with the sport itself serving as the driving force behind the plot and the main driver of the narrative. However, these films mostly use the sport as a backdrop to provide insight into the emotional arcs of the major characters and are not exclusively focused on the sport itself. Sports films frequently have allegories and can be dramatic or funny. The Bad News Bears (1976), A League of Their Own (1992), and Bend It Like Beckham (2003) are a few well-known sports films

12 - Thriller Genre

Thrillers skilfully combine suspense, tension, and mystery into one thrilling tale. Successful thrillers have a good pace, frequently include red herrings, reveal narrative twists, and expose information just when the audience needs to know it. A "ticking clock" element, where the stakes are against a limited amount of time, is a common feature of thrillers. The thriller subgenre includes crime flicks, political thrillers, and technological thrillers.

13 - Western Genre

In westerns, a cowboy or gunslinger chases an outlaw through the Wild West. Frequently, the main character will engage the villain in a duel or gunfight in the conclusion in order to exact revenge. The American West is shown in vivid plays called "westerns," where the desert, the mountains, or the plains can serve as both an inspiration for and an inspiration for the action. The Western genre has several subgenres, including spaghetti westerns, space westerns, and sci-fi westerns. Examples of Westerns include Django Unchained (2012) and The Good, the Bad, and the Ugly (1966).

4. Key Elements of Acting

4.1 Importance of Expressions in Acting

In acting, expressions are crucial because they are the main way that performers communicate to the audience the feelings, intentions, and thoughts of their characters. Actors use facial expressions extensively for the following reasons:

1. **Emotional Authenticity**: Actors can connect viscerally with the audience by bringing emotional authenticity to their performances through the use of expressions. Through the skilful use of facial expressions, body language, and vocal tone, actors may effectively convey emotions such as joy, grief, rage, or terror, so evoking empathy and resonance in the audience and bringing them into the narrative.

2. **Character Development and Depth**: By exposing their innermost feelings, motives, and vulnerabilities, actors' expressions assist in giving their characters nuance and complexity. Actors can convey complex facets of their characters' personalities and experiences through subtle facial expressions, gestures, and mannerisms, which improves the storyline and the audience's comprehension of it.

3. **Communication without Words**: Expressions frequently function as a kind of nonverbal communication that cuts over linguistic boundaries. Actors can convey a lot of information

and emotion through their facial expressions alone, even in scenes with little language. This makes for dramatic moments of comprehension and connection between characters and spectators.

4. **Engagement and Connection**: Throughout a performance, facial expressions are essential for drawing in and holding the attention of the audience. Exuberant and emotive performances enthral audiences, bringing them into the narrative and encouraging a feeling of empathy and involvement in the protagonists' adventures.

5. **Enhancements to Storytelling**: Expressions are vital instruments for improving the storytelling procedure. Actors employ facial expressions, such as a covert glance, a wry smile, or a tearful stare, to highlight important story elements, transmit subtext, and elicit certain emotional reactions from viewers, all of which enhance the narrative experience as a whole.

6. **Versatility and Adaptability**: In order to portray a wide range of characters and scenarios successfully, actors need to be fluid and adaptive in their use of expression. Actors need to have the flexibility to modify their facial expressions to fit the tone, style, and requirements of many types of performances, including comic and serious ones as well as historical epics and current dramas.

7. **Memorability and Impact**: The strength and impact of the actors' facial emotions are frequently what define memorable

performances. In both theatre and film, iconic moments are frequently characterized by the enduring impressions created by strong facial expressions that have an impact on both critics and viewers long after the performance has concluded.

Expressions are essentially the lifeblood of acting since they operate as a link between actors and audiences, a medium for the communication of emotions, and a means of revealing the emotional resonance and depth of a performance. Actors who have mastered the art of expression can take their performances to new heights and leave audiences with unforgettable memories.

4.2 IMPORTANCE OF BODY LANGUAGE IN ACTING

Acting requires body language, which is frequently regarded as just as important as spoken discourse. It entails expressing emotions, ideas, and intentions through posture, movement, and facial expressions. Actors can connect effectively with the audience during a performance by using body language to create credible characters and captivating narratives. The importance of body language in acting will be discussed in detail in this essay, along with its many facets, applications, and impacts on actors and spectators.

To start, one of the most important ways to portray emotions is through body language. Spoken words are useful for communicating information, but they are not always sufficient to fully express the nuance and complexity of human emotions. Here's where body language really shines since it gives actors a visceral, instantaneous way to portray emotions. For instance, clinched fists, stiff shoulders, and a wrinkled forehead can all effectively indicate rage or displeasure without the need for words. Similar to this, delicate and nuanced expressions of enjoyment or contentment can be conveyed with a soft smile, a relaxed posture, and gentle motions. Actors can enhance the authenticity and effectiveness of their performances by developing their body language skills, which allow them to access a vast reservoir of emotional expression.

Actors can develop fully complete personalities by using body language. Every person moves, gestures, and holds them self in a way that is specific to them and reflects their experiences, background, and personality. Because of this, performers need to become acutely aware of the different ways in which their characters would physically express themselves. This entails being aware of the motivations, history, and psychological composition of a character and expressing these things through their body language. A timid and insecure character, on the other hand, could hunch their shoulders and avoid making eye contact, while a confident and forceful character might walk across the stage with their head held high. Through the attention to these small nuances, actors may give their characters a sense of life and relatability to the viewer.

Actors can also communicate nonverbally with their scene companions by using body language. In many acting situations, gestures, facial emotions, and physical closeness play a big role in communication. This is especially true in private or highly charged scenes, where the depth of the individuals' connection or struggle may not be adequately conveyed by words alone. Actors may generate dynamic exchanges and establish rapport on stage or screen by observing the body language of their scene partner. Actors need to be extremely sensitive and responsive in order to adjust their own body language in real time in order to enhance and support their partner's performance.

Body language can be employed in a scenario to express hidden meanings and subtext. There are situations when silence can be just as significant as words uttered out loud. Actors can allude to underlying emotions, goals, and intentions by subtly altering their posture, facial expressions, and movements. This gives their performances greater nuance and complexity and encourages viewers to look past the obvious and get more involved with the narrative. For instance, a character might smile tightly and turn away from the recipient while making an apparently benign remark, alluding to hidden jealously or animosity. Actors may enhance the storytelling experience for both themselves and their audience by learning the craft of subtext and incorporating layers of meaning into their performances. Actors may enhance the storytelling experience for both themselves and their audience by learning the craft of subtext and incorporating layers of meaning into their performances.

Character relationships and power dynamics within a situation are conveyed through body language. Characters' physical interactions can disclose a lot about their roles, social standing, and sentiments toward one another. To demonstrate their power, a dominating character may, for example, make large movements and enter their scene partner's personal space, whilst a submissive character would draw back and avoid making direct eye contact. Actors may enhance the entire story and give their performances more depth by focusing on these dynamics and developing more genuine and captivating interactions between their characters.

Moreover, body language on stage or screen can be utilized to improve narrative and produce a striking visual effect. Actors are able to hold the attention of the audience, communicate important story points, and elicit strong emotional reactions by using expressive movement. This is especially crucial in silent films, dance, and physical theatre when the story mostly relies on visual imagery and there may be little to no spoken. Actors may engage and inspire audiences with dynamic and visually attractive performances by fully utilizing their bodies.

Additionally, body language is essential for expressing authenticity and cultural context throughout a performance. The rules, practices, and gestures that distinguish various cultures can have a significant impact on how people interact nonverbally. A handshake may be a customary greeting gesture in certain cultures but seen improper in others. Similarly, a head nod may indicate agreement in one culture but disapproval in another. In order to represent their roles in a believable and courteous manner, actors need to be aware of these cultural variations and adjust their body language accordingly. Research, empathy, and a willingness to learn about various cultural customs and viewpoints are necessary for this.

Body language can be an effective technique for physical embodiment and character development. Performers frequently go through rigorous training to hone their physicality and modify their bodies for specific roles. To properly embody a character, this may entail picking up particular movement styles, being proficient in a variety of physical manoeuvres, and even changing their posture, walk, and vocal tone. Actors can inhabit characters with authenticity and conviction by internalizing these physical changes via hard practice and rehearsal. This allows them to perform with these changes fluidly.

In conclusion, Actors can express emotions, develop characters, communicate nonverbally, convey subtext, build relationships, improve storytelling, convey cultural context, embody roles, and establish rhythm and pacing in a performance through the use of body language, which is a complex and vital component of acting. Actors can reach new heights in their performances by becoming adept at using body language to captivate viewers and vividly and compellingly bring characters and tales to life. Because of this, body language continues to be a fundamental component of the acting profession, providing countless opportunities for artistic expression.

4.3 What role has emotion got in acting?

Poor actors focus on their voice, as though speaking is the only way to express emotion. This frequently results in a throaty, choked tone that mimics the feeling of emotion. However, when we feel our emotions, it is a psychophysical event that involves vocal, physical, and mental responses and reactions. I'd venture to guess that the actor who makes an effort to sound as like they're attempting to express meaning by pushing their throat is actually feeling nothing. They are lying and cheating the audience, and it gets boring watching them.

However, actors should be able to embrace their emotions and use them to their advantage. Additionally, performers should not ignore their own emotions when playing out their roles because nothing an actor feels has any bearing on the circumstance.

When we behave in a way that is similar to the behaviour of the literary characters we wish to imitate, we will feel emotions, and we must be conscious of those emotions. The sheer desire to base our acting strategy on actual experience rather than genuine feeling does not diminish the significance of emotion in acting.

The bio-psychophysiological reaction to events that have an impact on us is called emotion. It can be seen both mentally and physically, and it never makes the same appearance twice. As a result, it is a very poor foundation upon which to create a character. Emotion is timid, uneasy, and uncontrollable; it cannot be prodded with a stick, and it will react in unexpected ways. The way Pavlov trained his dogs does not apply to training emotions. And even if you could, why would you want artificially triggered emotions? Their spontaneous emergence is what makes them beautiful.

I like to be a little less emotional in my acting since there aren't nearly enough performers in the UK who can pull off the correct emotion at the right time. They consequently mimic it, generally very poorly. Sadly, I would suggest that those who are able to experience one during rehearsal will concentrate on reliving that experience, which makes them more self-conscious, self-indulgent, and boring to watch on stage.

As actors, I'm sure you appreciate this aspect of your work, but I've never left a movie feeling inspired by an actor's ability to feel or express emotion. When a movie ends, I frequently find myself moved to silence. I am the one who is affected by it, and that's the key. When will I be moved? There are many instances, but I am typically impacted when a character with whom I have grown close or a link heroically endures something traumatic. Then I experience much more emotion than if I were to just sit and witness their tears.

5. NAVIGATING THE INDUSTRY

5.1 Auditions

In order to assess performers for certain roles in movies, TV series, plays, advertisements, and other projects, casting directors, producers, and directors use auditions, which are an essential part of the performing business. Actors can demonstrate their skill, range, and fit for a role or project during the audition process. This thorough explanation will examine the idea of auditions, including their importance, varieties, methods of preparation, and the dynamics that surround the auditioning process.

1. Significance of Auditions:

Actors can obtain roles in a variety of productions through auditions, which are an essential part of the casting process. They give casting directors the chance to evaluate an actor's physical presence, emotional range, acting prowess, and fit for a given role. Aside from that, auditions give actors a chance to show off their character interpretation, adaptability, and command of direction. In the end, casting directors and producers use auditions to gather information before making casting decisions so that the actors they choose will fit the project's vision.

2. Types of Auditions:

There are many different types of auditions, each designed to fit the needs and tastes of casting directors as well as the specifics of the production. Typical forms of auditions consist of:

- Cold Reading Auditions: In a cold reading audition, actors are required to play sequences from a script or sides (chosen scenes) without having read them through. In this kind of audition, an actor's spontaneity, adaptability, and speedy analysis and interpretation of the material are evaluated.

- Prepared Monologue Auditions: Actors select and prepare a monologue, or solo speech, from a play, movie, or other source for a prepared monologue audition. Actors can demonstrate their range, emotional nuance, and characterization talents in this kind of audition.

- Scripted Auditions: In this type of audition, prospective actors are given pre-rehearsed sequences or scenes from the production they are trying out for. Usually, they receive the material ahead of time, giving them time to be ready and practice before the audition. Scripted auditions evaluate an actor's ability to fully inhabit the role, carry off speech with conviction, and capture the right emotions and nuance of the moment.

- Improvisational Auditions: During an improvisational audition, actors must perform in an unscripted, impromptu manner in response to cues or scenarios that the casting panel provides. This kind of audition assesses an actor's improvisational abilities, originality, and quick thinking.

- Call-Back Auditions: Following an initial audition, actors who make the short list are invited back for a second assessment. To find the best actor for the part, call-back auditions frequently entail reading scenes with other actors, chemistry tests, or more scene work.

3. Techniques for Audition Preparation: In order to maximize performance and raise the chances of success, audition preparation is crucial. Among the practical pre-planning methods are:

- **Researching the Project**: Get acquainted with the project's themes, characters, genre, and tone. Gaining an understanding of the project's background will enable you to modify your performance to meet its needs.

- **Character Analysis**: Give the role you're trying out a close examination, going over their motives, relationships, personality, and past. Gain a thorough understanding of the character's psychology in order to represent them accurately.

- **Script Analysis**: Go over the script or audition sides in detail, focusing on the character dynamics, dialogue, subtext, and emotional moments. Determine the scene's important points and goals to guide your acting decisions.

- **Practice**: Give your audition material a lot of practice, either alone yourself or, if you can, with a scene partner. To discover the best performance, try delivering lines with alternative interpretations and experimenting with different emotions, gestures, and vocal accents.

- **Physical and Vocal Warm-Ups**: Warm up your body and voice for the audition by doing vocal and physical drills beforehand. In addition to reducing stress, stretching, breathing exercises, vocal exercises, and relaxation techniques can improve your presence and vocal clarity.

- **Building Confidence**: Use mindset exercises, visualization techniques, and positive affirmations to develop confidence in your acting abilities. Accept that anxiety is a normal part of the audition process and utilize it to your advantage by focusing your energy and enthusiasm.

4. Audition Process Dynamics: There are a number of important dynamics that affect an actor's experience and performance during the audition process, including:

- **Audition Setting**: There are many different types of audition settings, from small, private casting offices to busy rehearsal studios or theatre stages. Performers have to adjust to various environments and ambiances while being focused and attentive.

- **Casting Panel**: Directors, producers, casting directors, and occasionally writers or studio executives make up the casting panel. Actors have to manoeuvre around the complexities of the casting panel, building rapport and leaving a good impression all the while staying focused on their performance and acting professionally.

- **Direction and Feedback**: The casting panel may give actors directions or feedback during an audition. It's critical to be open to criticism, accept instructions with grace, and modify your performance as necessary. Exhibiting adaptability and a cooperative mindset can improve your chances of success.

- **Competition**: Actors compete fiercely for a small number of roles during auditions. Even if there can be fierce competition, actors should put more effort into presenting their individual talents and interpretations of the roles than they should into contrasting themselves with other actors.

- **Resilience**: Actors need to develop resilience in order to handle disappointments and failures, as rejection is a typical part of the audition process. All auditions offer a chance for development and education, no matter what happens.

In conclusion, auditions are an essential part of the performing business since they give performers the chance to showcase their skills, adaptability, and fit for particular parts. Success in the audition process depends on knowing the importance of auditions, being familiar with the various kinds, and using efficient preparation strategies. Actors can make the most of their possibilities and follow their dreams of becoming actors by handling the nuances of auditions with professionalism, confidence, and resiliency.

5.2 Who is a Film Director?

A film director, in my opinion, is the creative force behind the lens who transforms a screenplay into an emotionally charged and visually stunning work of art. Their distinctive combination of technical know-how, artistic vision, and leadership abilities steers all facet of the filmmaking process, from pre-production to post-production.

Film directors are storytellers who take viewers to new places, arouse feelings, and challenge preconceived notions using the language of film. Together, they work closely with editors, performers, cinematographers, and other crew members to realize their artistic vision for the screen. The responsibilities of a film director go beyond simple guidance; they are the ones who propel the creative vision of the picture, determining its tone, style, and impact as a whole. Through their talent, passion, and dedication, film directors have the power to leave a lasting legacy in the world of cinema.

5.3 Who is the Audience?

Actors believe that the audience is the ultimate platform for their creative expression and the beating heart of their craft. In addition to offering emotional resonance, criticism, and validation to the artistic endeavour, the audience is a representation of the people who watch and interpret the performances created by the performers.

The intensity and dynamism of live performances are shaped by the audience's responses and reactions, which actors see as active participants in the storytelling process. Whether on stage or film, depend on viewers to connect with their characters, identify with their challenges, and share in the narrative's emotional journey. Essentially, the audience is an essential component of the theatrical or cinematic experience, adding to the charm and force of storytelling by their participation and presence. They are not merely a passive observer.

6. PRACTICAL ASPECTS OF ACTING

6.1 9 Basic Acting Areas

The nine main performing areas, sometimes referred to as stage positions or zones, are essential ideas in theatre and performance that help directors and actors organize scenes more successfully. Regarding prominence, audience interaction, and dramatic effect, every place is unique.

We shall examine the traits, goals, and real-world uses of each of the nine fundamental acting domains in this thorough presentation.

1. **Centre Stage**: Arguably the most noticeable and central location on stage is the centre stage. It is positioned halfway between the breadth and depth of the stage, and it has great dramatic and symbolic significance. The major action of a scene usually takes place in the centre, where important moments also happen and where the main characters are drawn to. The main actors in a performance dominate the audience's attention and communicate the main themes or conflicts. Furthermore, centre stage provides the audience with the best visibility, guaranteeing that important moments are not missed.

2. **Centre Stage Right**: From the performers' point of view facing the audience, centre stage right is the region immediately to the right of centre stage. Character interactions or the introduction of supporting characters or plotlines usually take place in this zone. Centre stage right is somewhat prominent and visible,

however not as prominent as centre stage. By acting as a link between the main point and the stage's edges, actors positioned in this area can interact with both the audience and centre stage.

3. **Centre Stage Left**: Centre stage left takes up the area on the left side that is next to centre stage, much like centre stage right does. It fulfils similar functions in terms of performance and staging. In order to create dynamic stage compositions and ease the flow of action across the stage, actors positioned in centre stage left frequently interact with those in centre stage right. Similar to its opposite, centre stage left keeps some visibility and importance, which facilitates strong character development and narrative.

4. **Downstage Centre**: The front and middle portion of the stage, nearest to the audience, is referred to as downstage centre. Actors are in close proximity to the audience, which increases intimacy and connection. Because of its close closeness to the audience, downstage centre is frequently utilized for intimate, confrontational, or highly charged moments in a performance. A sense of immediacy and involvement can be fostered by actors who take up downstage centre and make direct eye contact with the audience.

5. **Downstage Right**: From the performers' point of view as they face the audience, downstage right is the front-right portion of the stage. Downstage right provides a little different view than downstage centre, although it is still quite near to the audience. This space is frequently used to show character interactions or

to draw attention to particular language or actions. Downstage right actors have the opportunity to interact with the audience as well as their scene partners, using the stage's spatial dynamics to improve characterization and storytelling.

6. **Downstage Left**: Taking up the front-left portion of the stage, downstage left is mirrored by downstage right. Similar to its opposite, downstage left gives a clear view point for staging situations and is close to the audience. This space works well for a variety of dramatic objectives, such as character interactions, entrances, and exits. By utilizing the spatial dynamics of the stage, actors positioned downstage left can effectively portray emotions, intents, and relationships. This allows for the creation of engaging performances.

7. **Upstage Centre**: The back and middle section of the stage, furthest away from the spectators, is referred to as upstage centre. In the past, the upstage area's distance from the audience made it less appealing, which decreased visibility and effect. But modern staging methods have made upstage centre a practical and adaptable performing space. When characters go back from the foreground of the action for periods of contemplation, introspection, or solitude, upstage centre is frequently utilized. The gap between them and the audience allows actors positioned upstage centre to express depth, subtlety, and emotion.

8. **Upstage Right**: Mirroring downstage right's location, upstage right takes up the rear-right portion of the stage. Upstage right provides special chances for staging and performance, although being generally linked with less visibility and significance. This space can be utilized for character placement in relation to the main action or for entrances and exits. The spatial dynamics of the stage can be used by actors positioned upstage right to add depth, dimension, and visual interest, which improves the overall composition of scenes.

9. **Upstage Left**: Upstage left occupies the rear-left portion of the stage and is mirrored by Upstage Right. Similar to its opposite, upstage left presents chances for clever character placement and staging. This space can be used for a number of things, like establishing asymmetry, bringing attention to particular parts of a scene, or balancing stage compositions. Upstage left actors are able to interact with other characters or set pieces while being somewhat apart from the audience, which enhances performance complexity and subtlety.

To sum up, the nine fundamental acting zones cover a variety of on-stage postures and viewpoints, each of which fulfils a distinct purpose in terms of visibility, dramatic effect, and narrative. Directors and performers may create visually stunning, captivating, and dynamic performances that captivate audiences by knowing and leveraging these areas. Theatre professionals can give stories depth, authenticity, and theatricality by grasping the spatial dynamics of the stage and placing characters and actions in strategic ways.

6.2 ACTING TIPS

Of course! The following are some excellent pointers for performers who want to improve:

1. **Study the Craft**: To advance your knowledge of acting theory, methods, and techniques, enrol in acting seminars, workshops, and courses.

2. **Watch and Learn**: Take in the acting performances of seasoned performers in plays, television series, and motion pictures. Examine their methods, personas, and subtleties to get knowledge from their experience.

3. **Practice Often**: Set aside time to work on scenes, monologues, and acting exercises to hone your performance abilities and boost your self-esteem.

4. **Develop Emotional Range**: Investigate many emotions and gain the ability to access and express them truthfully as you work to broaden your emotional range.

5. **Develop Vocal Skills**: Concentrate on vocal exercises to enhance your voice's emotional resonance, projection, and clarity. Delivering performances that are captivating requires a voice that is well-trained.

6. **Focus on physique**: To accurately portray your character's physique and presence on stage or screen, pay attention to your posture, gestures, and body language.

7. **Develop Character Depth**: To create fully realized and nuanced performances, take the time to analyse and develop your characters. This includes learning about their motives, backstories, and relationships.

8. **Embrace Vulnerability**: Don't be scared to show your emotions during performances and to be vulnerable. Honesty and authenticity are essential for building rapport with audiences.

9. **Seek Feedback**: Ask colleagues, directors, and acting coaches for their opinions. You may hone your craft and discover areas for development with the aid of constructive criticism.

10. **Remain Patient and Persistent**: Acting is a demanding and cutthroat industry, so maintain your patience and dedication to your work. Acting success frequently involves tenacity, fortitude, and a desire to develop and learn new skills.

You can improve your ability to enthral audiences with your skill and creativity and further develop as a performer by applying these suggestions to your acting practice.

6.3 ACTING AT HOME: A GUIDE TO PRACTICE

For those who want to be actors, learning how to practice acting at home can be a rewarding experience. Acting at home has several advantages, regardless of your experience level. Whether you're a novice trying to improve your abilities or an experienced performer hoping to enhance your trade. I'll go over a variety of methods, exercises, tools, and advice in this extensive guide to help you improve your acting from the comforts of home.

Knowing the Fundamentals of Acting

It's important to comprehend the fundamentals of acting before delving into particular exercises and approaches. The art of acting is accurately and convincingly interpreting a role. To provide an engaging performance, it entails taking on the character's feelings, attitudes, and actions. Here are some essential ideas to understand:

1. **Character Analysis**: It's essential to be real to grasp the desires, motivations, and past of the character you're playing.

2. **Emotional Truth**: To effectively act, one must be able to communicate authentic feelings to the audience.

3. **Physicality**: A character's posture, gestures, and use of space can all give away a lot about their motivations and nature.

4. **Voice and Speech**: Characterization and communication can be improved by using voice modulation, diction, and speech patterns effectively.

5. **Imagination and Creativity**: To give characters life and construct plausible situations, actors frequently rely on their imaginations.

Setting Up Your Home Acting Space

For effective practice sessions, it's important to create a welcoming atmosphere. Here are some pointers for arranging your living room for acting:

1. **Quiet Environment**: Select a place where you can concentrate without being disturbed that is calm and free of distractions.

2. **Plenty of Room**: Make sure you have plenty space to walk around comfortably, particularly if you want to engage in any physical activities or situations.

3. **Appropriate Lighting**: Good lighting is essential for mood setting and visibility. Lamps with adjustable shades or natural light might be useful.

4. **Props and Costumes**: Collect any accessories or outfits that could improve your acting or help you immerse yourself in the role.

5. **Recording Equipment**: You might want to film your rehearsals using a camera or smartphone. Rewatching a recording can yield insightful information for advancement.

Warm-Up Exercises

It's important to warm up your voice and body before beginning scene work or a monologue. These exercises improve your flexibility, help you relax your muscles, and help you get mentally ready for the acting that lies ahead. Consider attempting these warm-up exercises:

1. **Physical Warm-Up**: To increase flexibility and release tense muscles, begin with light stretches. Incorporate full-body exercises like Tai Chi or yoga.

2. **Voice Warm-Up**: Work on your articulation, resonance, and projection by doing vocal exercises. Vocal scales, breathing techniques, and tongue twisters can all help warm up your voice.

3. **Emotional Warm-Up**: Give yourself some time to connect with your feelings and experience a range of emotions. Consider your own experiences or engage in sensory activities to elicit particular emotions.

Acting Exercises and Techniques

After warming up, it's time to start acting exercises and techniques that will advance your abilities. You should include the following successful techniques in your at-home acting routine:

1. **Character Development**: Pick a character from a play, movie, or book, and learn everything you can about their personality, motives, and past. Make a character diary or notebook to record their feelings and ideas.

2. **Practice Your Monologues**: Choose and practice your favourite monologues extensively. Pay attention to the character's goals, rhythms, and changes in emotion throughout the speech.

3. **Scene Study**: Collaborate on scenes from plays or screenplays with a friend or member of your family. Focus on the dynamics of relationships, goals, and characters.

4. **Improvisation**: You may improve your ability to think quickly, respond truthfully, and become more spontaneous as an actor by practicing improvisation. Practice creating scenes, situations, or dialogue between characters on the fly.

5. **Sensory Work**: To strengthen your bond with your characters and environment, use your senses. Investigate how your character's experience is influenced by noises, tastes, scents, and textures by doing sensory activities.

6. **Practice Your Voice and Speech**: Set aside time for voice and speech exercises to enhance vocal diversity, clarity, and resonance. To broaden your range, try out several accents, dialects, and voice characteristics.

7. **Emotional Readiness**: Acquire methods for genuinely feeling and expressing a variety of emotions. To elicit real emotional reactions, engage in emotional recall, sensory memory, and visualization exercises.

Resources for Practice Acting at Home

You may support your home acting endeavours with a plethora of materials in addition to practicing alone. Here are some recommendations:

1. **Online Workshops and Classes**: A lot of respectable acting schools and teachers provide online workshops and classes on a variety of subjects, from audition preparation to acting approaches.

2. **Books and guidelines**: Examine acting theory, method, and practice books, guidelines, and textbooks. Seek out materials written by well-known acting instructors and professionals.

3. **Online Videos and Tutorials**: Websites such as YouTube provide a plethora of free-acting exercises, tutorials, and guidance from professionals in the field.

4. **Scripts and Monologue Collections**: You can obtain scene snippets, scripts, and monologue collections online or in your neighbourhood library. Select reading that piques your curiosity and challenges you.

5. **Virtual Acting Communities**: To network with other actors, exchange resources, and get critiques on your work, sign up for online discussion boards, social media groups, or virtual acting communities.

Advice for Efficient Practice at Home

Take into account the following advice to get the most out of your at-home acting practice sessions:

1. **Consistency**: Create a practice schedule that you stick to on a regular basis. Over time, even brief practice sessions can produce noticeable gains.

2. **Put Process First**: Rather of obsessing about quick fixes or results, embrace the process of learning and development. Savour the process of learning about and honing your craft.

3. **Feedback and Reflection**: To get insightful criticism on your performances, ask acting coaches, peers, or trustworthy mentors for their opinions. Consider your accomplishments and your room for development.

4. **Have an Open Mind**: Continue to be receptive to attempting novel methods, strategies, and tasks. Accept experimentation and exploration as essential components of education.

5. **Take Breaks**: To avoid burnout and preserve your enthusiasm for your craft, allow yourself to take breaks when necessary.

6. **Celebrate Your Success**: No matter how modest, recognize and honour your accomplishments. Acknowledge your development and improvement as an actor.

Conclusion

You can improve your acting abilities at your own pace and convenience by practicing at home. It can be a fulfilling and enriching experience. You can improve your skills and increase your love for the art by learning the principles of acting, setting up a comfortable acting area at home, doing warm-up exercises, experimenting with different acting exercises and approaches, making use of resources, and adhering to practical practice advice. Keep in mind that acting is a lifetime learning and development process, so seize any chance to broaden your horizons and let your creative side show.

6.4 How any actor should spend their entire day

Creating a detailed daily schedule for an actor takes into account many facets of their personal and professional lives. Every hour of the day, from the moment they wake up until they go to bed, is an opportunity to improve their skill, foster relationships, and take care of their physical and mental health.

Here's a detailed breakdown:

Morning Schedule (6:00 AM - 8:00 AM)

An actor usually starts their day early in order to prepare and ponder during the peaceful times. Establishing the tone for the day ahead is largely dependent on the morning routine. Usually, it begins with:

1. **Wake Up**: Actors who rise early are able to cultivate a disciplined mindset and enjoy the peace of the morning.

2. **Exercise**: Getting moving, whether it be through weight training, yoga, or jogging, not only maintains the body in shape but also energizes the mind and improves mood.

3. **Meditation or mindfulness**: Making time for these activities helps cultivate emotional resilience, mental clarity, and focus— all of which are critical for overcoming the obstacles faced by those working in the entertainment sector.

4. **voice Warm-Ups**: Actors who want to give strong performances on stage or screen need to maintain voice health, clarity, and projection. Vocal exercises help with this.

5. **Nutritious Breakfast**: Providing the body with a healthy breakfast helps to ensure that energy levels remain high all day.

Professional Development and Networking (8:00 AM - 12:00 PM)

Actors spend the first portion of the day networking and developing their careers after finishing their morning ritual. During this time, there are activities like:

1. **Script Analysis**: The foundation for honest depiction during auditions and performances is laid by devoting time to script analysis, character analysis, and motivational analysis.

2. **Acting Classes or Workshops**: In order to hone their craft, discover fresh approaches, and maintain relevance in a cutthroat field, actors must pursue ongoing education. Participating in acting workshops or seminars offers you the chance to improve and get advice from knowledgeable teachers.

3. **Auditions or Casting Calls**: Going to an audition or casting call needs a lot of planning. You need to learn your lines by heart, study the character and the project, and show up as the confident, real version of the role.

4. **Meetings with Agents or Managers**: Establishing and sustaining relationships with agents or managers entails keeping lines of communication open, talking about professional objectives, planning out opportunities, and resolving any issues that may arise.

Lunch and Self-Care (12:00 PM - 1:00 PM)

Lunch breaks are crucial for recharging the body and mind. During this period, actors take care of their physical and mental needs by engaging in self-care activities like:

1. **Healthy Meal**: Eating a balanced meal gives you the nutrition you need and keeps your energy levels up for the rest of the day.

2. **Mindful Break**: Refreshing the mind and reducing stress can be achieved by taking a little break to relax, whether it be by deep breathing, meditation, or just taking in the surroundings.

3. **Hydration**: Maintaining adequate hydration is essential to general health and wellbeing. Actors make it a priority to stay hydrated throughout the day in order to perform at their best.

Rehearsals or Shoots (1:00 PM - 6:00 PM)

For ongoing projects, the afternoon is frequently devoted to rehearsals or photo sessions. Intense concentration, teamwork, and creative investigation define this time:

1. **Rehearsals**: Whether for a theatre production, a movie, or a television show, rehearsals give actors the chance to hone their performances, investigate character relationships, and collaborate closely with directors and other members of the cast.

2. **On-Set Preparation**: To guarantee a seamless shoot, performers working in film or television projects must become acquainted with the set, blocking, and camera angles. They must also work in tandem with the production crew.

3. **Performance**: Actors use their imagination and preparation to produce captivating performances, remain in the present, and react to their surroundings and fellow actors in an authentic manner while filming sequences.

4. **Feedback and Adjustments**: During rehearsals or filming, actors can improve their performances, make the necessary changes, and aim for greatness by soliciting feedback from directors, coaches, or fellow performers.

Dinner and Social Engagement (6:00 PM - 8:00 PM)

As the workweek comes to an end, performers turn their attention to personal fulfilment and social engagement:

1. **Dinner with Friends or Family**: Eating with close friends and family members offers a chance for bonding, unwinding, and having fun away from job commitments.

2. **Cultural Events or Networking**: Actors can maintain professional connections, immerse themselves in creative inspiration, and stay in touch with their colleagues by going to cultural events, movie screenings, or industry networking events.

3. **Personal Projects or Hobbies**: Taking up writing, painting, or music making are examples of personal projects or hobbies

that foster creativity and offer a welcome means of self-expression apart from performing.

Evening Routine and Relaxation (8:00 PM - 10:00 PM)

Actors wind down and get ready for rejuvenating slumber when night falls:

1. **Wind-Down Routine**: Creating a soothing bedtime ritual, like journaling, reading, or a warm bath, tells the body and mind that it's time to wind down.

2. **Reflection**: Taking stock of the day's successes, setbacks, and thankful moments helps maintain perspective and emotional stability.

3. **Sleep Preparation**: Creating a comfortable sleeping environment, cutting down on screen time, and using relaxation techniques are all important sleep hygiene habits that should be prioritized in order to achieve restful and rejuvenating sleep.

In summary, an actor's day is a meticulously planned fusion of work-related obligations, personal growth, and self-care. Actors can build a successful and long-lasting career in the entertainment industry by putting their profession first, taking care of their relationships, and keeping everything in balance.

7. Character Development

7.1 Strategies for character development.

Character development is the process of generating believable and complex characters in a story. Good character development can get readers spellbound by a narrative. For any written art that you may be working on, including novels, films or short stories, strong characters are core to engaging storytelling. In this tutorial, we shall show different ways of developing your characters so as to make them appealing and memorable.

Understanding Your Characters

1. **Character Profiles**: For each main character, generate specific details such as his/her past life, personality traits, reasons behind their behaviour/actions/motivations; strength points and weaknesses plus likes or dislikes and fears they have. This will help develop who they are guiding their actions throughout your story.

2. **Backstory**: Create a deep backstory for each of your characters. This involves exploring their previous interactions with other people as well as important happenings in their lives. Knowing where the protagonist comes from helps in understanding why he/she acts the way they do.

3. **Character Arcs**: Develop character arcs that depict how your protagonists grow through adversity during their journey across the book's pages. What beliefs will change about them? What values are held before being forced to face obstacles?

4. **Motivation and goals**: What are the motivations and aims of your characters? Make it clear. What do they want for themselves, and why do they want that? This will make them act to achieve their desires and create a story around.

Creating Believable Characters

1. **Complexity** – Avoid single dimensional characters by infusing them with complexity and depth. They should be real people, exhibiting multiple traits, quirks, and contradictions among others. Realistic personality flaws make readers relate to the characters more closely.

2. **Empathy** – Create characters who readers can empathize with by showcasing their vulnerabilities, struggles as well as their humanity. By demonstrating the emotional and psychological dimensions of what they go through, you will establish connection with your audience.

3. **Unique Voice** – Each character must have his or her unique voice which reveals his or her own personality, background, perspective on life etcetera in a way of speaking as well as mannerism that is peculiar to him or her only. Take note of dialogue and speech patterns in order to differentiate between characters' voices and bring them alive on paper.

4. **Consistency** – Be consistent concerning the behaviour, thoughts, actions demonstrated by your characters throughout the story. For believability's sake ensure that every decision made by protagonists has its roots within their established traits as well as motives till the end of this narrative piece.

Methods of Creating Characters

1. **Observation**: Make characters that are both true to life and impersonations of them by drawing from the real world and personal experiences. Watch how people react, speak, and express themselves in different circumstances and include these nuances in your writing.

2. **Interviewing Characters**: Pose questions to your imaginary subjects during a conversation so as to attempt an understanding of them more fully in terms of their nature, background or underlying reasons for doing certain things. Let them answer the questions and understand who they are as well as what motivates their actions.

3. **Character Exercises**: Try things like journal entries from character's perspectives; write scenes from their past; imagine a situation involving them so as to study their reactions and thoughts.

4. **Psychological Profiling**: You can use this method to develop character definition through profiling behaviour or personalities with psychological techniques. Find out about something like MBTI personality types, Enneagram types, or attachment styles which will give you insights into your characters' minds based on such factors.

Show, Don't Tell

1. **Actions and Reactions**: Your characters' behaviours, responses, and social interactions reveal their personalities. Show the reader what a character is like by their actions and decisions rather than just telling them.

2. **Internal Monologue**: Use introspection and internal monologue to reveal the feelings and thoughts of your characters. To help the reader better understand them, reveal their inner conflicts, uncertainties, and wants.

3. **Dialogue and Subtext**: Highlight character motivations, tensions, and interactions through dialogue and subtext. Observe the silences between characters and the ways in which their statements reveal their true motivations and emotions.

4. **Symbolism and Metaphor**: To reveal more nuanced aspects of your characters' motivations, use symbolism and metaphor in your narrative. Reflect their inner states and thematic meaning through the use of objects, locations, and imagery.

Development and Expansion

1. **Challenges and Obstacles**: Put your characters through hardships that compel them to face their fears, face their convictions, and develop as people. Character growth and story advancement are fuelled by conflict.

2. **develop and Transformation**: Give your characters room to grow and develop as a result of their encounters with the plot and its events. Demonstrate how their priorities, viewpoints, and relationships develop throughout time.

3. **Resolution and Closure**: By addressing your characters' goals, problems, and personal development by the conclusion of the story, you may bring your characters' arcs to a satisfying conclusion. Assure them of a sense of catharsis or completion that meets their goals on the outside as well as their interior journey.

4. **Ongoing Development**: Take into account how your characters' life will carry on after the last few pages of the novel are closed. Give readers the freedom to imagine and make their own assumptions about the futures of your characters by giving them space to do so.

Conclusion

The process of developing a character is dynamic and continuous, requiring meticulous preparation, observation, and implementation. You may develop characters that ring true with readers, arouse empathy and emotion, and advance the story with nuance and authenticity by utilizing these methods and strategies. Don't forget to put in the time and effort to comprehend the motivations of your characters, develop likable personalities, and depict their development as the plot progresses. You can make your characters come to life and draw readers into their quests for understanding, growth, and atonement if you put in the effort and use your imagination.

7.2 Comprehending Character Arcs

Character arcs are the transformative journeys that characters undergo over the course of a story. From their initial state to their ultimate destination, character arcs trace the evolution of a character's beliefs, motivations, and behaviour. Understanding character arcs is essential for creating dynamic and compelling characters that resonate with audiences.

In this guide, we'll explore:

1. The different types of character arcs
2. The elements that comprise them
3. Techniques for crafting effective arcs in storytelling

Types of Character Arcs

There are three main types of character arcs:

1. **Positive Arc**: A protagonist with a positive character arc starts the story with defects, constraints, or inner conflicts that prevent them from growing. They face these difficulties throughout the story, experience personal growth, and come out of it a stronger, more mature version of themselves. A self-realization or epiphany that results in good change is frequently the culmination of positive arcs.

2. **Negative Arc**: On the other hand, a negative character arc tracks the protagonist's decline toward moral decay or darkness. As the story goes on, the character may have good intentions or traits at first, but they eventually give in to their weaknesses,

temptations, or outside forces. A moment of reckoning or self-destruction is a common conclusion of negative arcs, which leave the character radically altered, usually in a negative way.

3. **Flat Arc**: In a flat character arc, the protagonist provides a steady anchor for the story's shifting events by staying essentially the same throughout. The fundamental identity, values, and beliefs of the flat character never change, even while their surroundings do. In ensemble storylines or narratives where the protagonist acts as a catalyst for other characters' changes, flat arcs are frequently used.

Elements of Character Arcs

Understanding the essential components of character arcs is crucial if you want to write them in your stories successfully:

1. **Starting Point**: Every character arc has a beginning point, a starting moment that marks the beginning of the character's transformational journey. The character's beginning states are established, along with their motives, beliefs, flaws, and emotional baggage.

2. **Inciting Incident**: The inciting incident is what starts the character's arc by upsetting their normal routine and drawing them into the conflict of the story. The inciting incident, whether it be a catastrophe, an unexpected meeting, or a realization that alters the course of the character's life, compels the persona to face their shortcomings and set out on a quest for self-awareness.

3. **Challenges and difficulties**: The character is put to the test by a number of difficulties and challenges they encounter throughout the narrative, which try their fortitude, resiliency, and resourcefulness. These challenges can be internal (doubts, anxieties, or traumatic experiences from the past) or external (agonists, conflicts, or physical hurdles), but they are all meant to drive the character to step outside of their comfort zone and undergo growth.

4. **Transformational Moments**: Important turning points in a character's journey that signify notable changes in their attitudes, beliefs, or conduct are interspersed throughout character arcs. These can be epiphanies, conflicts, giving up something, or victorious events that move the character one step closer to their goal.

5. **Climax**

The climax of the character arc is the culmination of the protagonist's journey, where they:

* Confront their inner demons
* Face their greatest fears
* Make a pivotal decision that defines their character

This is the moment of truth for the character, where their arc reaches its dramatic peak and their fate hangs in the balance.

6. Resolution

Following the climax, the character experiences resolution—a sense of closure or completion that reflects the outcome of their arc. This resolution can take various forms, depending on the type of arc and the narrative context:

* Positive arcs may conclude with a moment of redemption or personal growth
* Negative arcs may end in tragedy or moral decay.

Crafting Effective Character Arcs

1. **Character Development**: Begin by creating multifaceted, fully realized characters with unique personalities, objectives, and weaknesses. Recognize the motivations of your characters and how they will change as the story progresses.

2. **Describe the Arc**: Describe the course of your character's arc, including its beginning, major turning points, and end. Think about the ways in which the character's arc relates to the story's overall plot and thematic components.

3. **Foreshadowing and Set-Up**: Use character dynamics, subliminal signals, or foreshadowing to sow the seeds of future development early in the narrative. Establish the foundation for the character's journey so that it feels natural and well-earned.

4. **Emotional resonance**: Make an emotional connection with your character's journey by drawing from universal themes, feelings, and experiences that people can relate to. Permit viewers or readers to identify personally with the character's hardships and victories.

5. **Internal Conflict**: Examine the conflicts, anxieties, uncertainties, and wants that your character is experiencing internally. Characters with internal turmoil have greater nuance and complexity in their arcs, which enhances the appeal and relatability of their journey.

6. **Arc Reversals**: To keep the audience interested and challenge their assumptions, include unexpected turns or reversals in your character's arc. Push the character's arc in new directions by challenging their beliefs or making them face painful realities.

Examples of Character Arcs in Literature and Film

1. **Positive Arc**: One good arc is that of Frodo Baggins, who in "The Lord of the Rings" progresses from being a reluctant hero crippled by self-doubt to a brave leader prepared to give his all-in order to preserve Middle-earth.

2. **Negative Arc**: Walter White from "Breaking Bad" moves from being a polite chemistry teacher to a vicious drug lord driven by avarice and power. This is an example of a negative arc.

3. **Flat Arc**: Despite the racial biases and social injustices he encounters in the divided South, Atticus Finch in "To Kill a

Mockingbird" exemplifies a flat arc by sticking to his moral convictions.

Conclusion

Character arcs are the backbone of compelling storytelling, offering audiences insight into the transformative journeys of fictional characters. By understanding the different types of character arcs, the elements that comprise them, and techniques for crafting effective arcs, writers can create dynamic and relatable characters that resonate with audiences on a deep emotional level.

Character arcs provide a framework for exploring themes of growth, redemption, and self-discovery, enriching the narrative experience and leaving a lasting impact on readers or viewers.

8. Improvisation

8.1 The value of improvisational abilities in acting.

The technique of generating scenarios, language, and actions on the spot without reading from a script or memorizing lines is known as improvisation in acting. In order to generate authentic and compelling performances, actors respond quickly to signals, situations, or other actors. They rely on their creativity, intuition, and capacity for cooperation.

Actors frequently use improvisation to build scenes, delve into characters, and enhance spontaneity and authenticity. It may occur during workshops, lectures, or rehearsals. It forces artists to embrace the erratic character of live performance and to be quick-witted and adaptable.

Both a technique and an art form, improvisation is used in performance. Without the confines of a text, actors can explore characters and relationships in novel and unexpected ways. It enables individuals to establish a connection with their imagination, spontaneity, and instincts.

One essential element of improvisation is active listening. To respond authentically, actors must be completely present and aware of the cues, gestures, and language used by their scene partners. Collaboration fosters spontaneity and connection, which makes for engaging and exciting performances.

It's encouraged for actors to improvise freely and trust their creative impulses. They don't follow a script; instead, they follow their creativity and intuition, embracing surprise and vulnerability in the moment. This willingness to take chances can lead to spontaneous and creative outbursts that captivate onlookers. Additionally, helpful for character development is improvisation.

Through improvisation, actors can explore a range of facets related to the personalities, motivations, and relationships of their characters. Their understanding of the character is improved and their performance is guided by this process of discovery.

Improvisation is useful in acting in addition to its artistic benefits. It can solve technical issues, revive performances, and close pacing gaps in the screenplay. Improvisation is very helpful in audition situations where actors may have to respond to unanticipated signals or perform cold readings.

Improvisation promotes teamwork and group projects. Through sharing ideas and contributions, actors create a joyful and imaginative mood and a sense of communal responsibility for the performance. This cooperative approach not only enhances the calibre of the performance but also promotes friendship and respect between the actors.

All things considered.

Overall, an actor's toolkit includes improvisation as a valuable and significant technique. It enables artists to tap into their creativity, spontaneity, and intuition, producing engaging and authentic performances. Through improvisation, actors can experiment with new concepts and push the limits of their art, improving both the audience's and their own performing experience.

8.2 Games and Activities involving improvisation

Drama schools, drama workshops, team building activities, and improv comedy shows are some of the places where these games are used to help foster improvisational skills, confidence, creative expression among other things as well with actors encouraged to work together on them as part of being creative or spontaneous. In this book there will be various types of improv games explored suitable for individuals at any level or age group.

Warm-Up Exercises

1. **Zip Zap Zop**: Participates parting each other with imaginary energy balls during this where this is done by forming a circle and repeating the word 'zip' as you pass them. The speed should be moderate in such a way that everyone can manage it comfortably. The main aim for it should be to make sure that you are able to do without losing out on the best way to go about getting near someone else for warmer energy balls throwing exchange.

2. **Mirror Exercise**: Have the participants pair off and face each other in the activity area. One person should take charge while the other follows by copying every move made by the leader slowly and deliberately. Encourage them to focus on synchronization and nonverbal communication alone.

3. **Sound ball**: For this activity, the team members should form a circle by standing up. One of them will start with a "sound ball" which is an imaginary object passed around through clapping, humming or snapping. Before giving it to someone else, every player must add his/her unique sound.

Character Building Games

1. One-character swap game can be played where people are placed into pairs and are asked to come up with different individuals who have unique characteristics, mannerisms and ways of talking. They then work on a scene together switching their parts around from time to time so that they can see how well each person can adapt.

2. A "Guess the Character" game may involve one player taking up the role of a famous person in secret while others try to find out who it is by asking questions about historical figures, books or movies.

3. During "Character Walks" exercises players should move around an area using big steps, specific postures and hand movements that reflect different personalities. They should also be asked to interchange between different types of people with unique physical attributes and ways of being.

Scene Work Games

1. Each player contributes a word eventually making up a story told one word at a time. Sharing this experience of game playing helps encourage quick thinking, creativity and teamwork.

2. Participants have to act out short scenes using only three words each time they speak. Players must be able to get their point across clearly and concisely while maintaining the flow of the scene when engaged in this kind of gaming activity.

3. After acting in a certain style or category such as science fiction, romance etc.; the teacher will call another one out while the students are still performing. Flexibility is one thing that performance is required to have in this kind of game.

Improv Comedy Games

1. Scene Replay: When two participants do a quick scene, a facilitator shouts to stop and picks another person to play out the scene differently. This activity encourages quick thinking and being spontaneous.

2. Lines from a Hat: Individuals write down sentences or phrases on sheets of paper, which are then placed into a container such as a hat. During the performance, players pick out words randomly from the container and incorporate them into their lines. What does this activity do to a scene?

3. Party Quirks: One person holds a party, and the rest act as strange guests with different quirks or identities. The host has to figure out who is who based on the way they interact. This game fosters imagination and comic sense of timing.

Storytelling Games

1. **Story Circle**: Participants take turns sitting in a circle to add their part to a group story. Each person, while developing the thoughts of others, offers a sentence or two for the story. Thus, all participants have the opportunity to show their creativity in presenting and participate in the work of each other during the task. Storytelling skills, team participation, and collaboration are encouraged in this game.

2. **Story Spine**: The players jointly compose an arbitrary structure comprising the "story spine." Here, each participant has to say the following line. "Once upon a time… Every day… But one day… Because of that… Because of that… Until finally… And ever since then" are the lines that the participants must say in turn. This game encourages players to build stories with meaning and have a logical beginning, middle, and end.

3. **Genre Roulette**: Players make up a story as they go, and the facilitator shouts out different types that they should put in the story with their own tradition and style, like western, fantasy, and mystery players. Players of this game need to control their storytelling to merge fashionable genre elements and elements with the tradition and style of their production.

Anyone who employs actors, performers, or audience members of all ages and abilities can gain from improvisation fun and activities which contribute to whim, ingenuity, and collaboration. They are used for storytelling, improv entree, identity building, warm-up practices, or page works to encourage players to respond and grasp the unexpected significance and the option to be creative.

8.3 Including improvisation in moments that are scripted.

Performances in a number of medias, inclusive of theatre, tv, and cinema, can gain depth, spontaneity, and authenticity via incorporating improvisation into pre-written scenes. Although actors have a shape to function within throughout scripted sequences, improvisation gives them the freedom to feature their own imagination and spontaneity to the action, giving it a more herbal and vibrant feel. This guide will cowl the advantages of the use of improvisation in deliberate scenes, the way to combine improvised and scripted aspects together obviously, and a hit integration in a variety of media.

Benefits of Incorporating Improvisation

1. **Increased Authenticity**: Actors react organically to the emotions and dynamics of the state of affairs at some stage in improvisation, which lends scripted moments a more genuine nice. Audiences may be moved by means of those actual, emotionally charged moments that are produced via this spontaneity.

2. **Character Exploration**: Actors can cross similarly into their characters through improvisation, examining their relationships, motivations, and emotional states inside the second. The characters' layers of complexity may be introduced and the performance improved by way of this process of discovery.

3. **Dynamic Performances**: By including improvisation, indicates can advantage vitality and dynamic that keeps them interesting and fascinating for each performers and visitors. Using improvisation, performers can discover new alternatives and observe their instincts, giving scripted scenes a fresh perspective.

4. **Collaborative Process**: Actors, administrators, and writers can work collectively to find the most enticing and a hit way to bring the scene to lifestyles when you consider that improvisation creates collaborative surroundings. Novel storytelling strategies and innovative breakthroughs can end result from this collaborative technique.

Techniques for Blending Scripted and Improvised Moments

1. **Establish Clear bounds**: To ensure that improvisation provides to instead of takes far away from the scenario, definitely outline the constraints and bounds before introducing it into scripted parts. Ascertain which elements of the scenario can be improvised and which want to be scripted.

2. **Keep Your Focus on Your Goals**: When improvising, performers should keep their interest at the scripted goals and intentions of their characters. Instead of going off on beside the point tangents, improvisation ought to increase the emotional fact of the character and flow the tale along.

3. **Listen and React**: Active listening and prompt responses to other actors' alerts and movements are important to improvisation. Actors must be advocated to improvise their strains and movements whilst closing in the gift and responding genuine to the scene's dynamics.

4. **Accept Mistakes**: Acknowledge the unpredictable nature of improvisation and provide room for errors or unanticipated occasions to take place. Sometimes improvisation and spontaneity bring about the most powerful and memorable scenes.

5. **Practice and Experiment**: Allow actors to try out numerous strategies and procedures all through rehearsals via inclusive of improvisation. Actors can also sense more comfortable and assured when improvising instantaneous during real performances if they undergo this practice session manner.

Examples of Incorporating Improvisation

1. **Movie**: Matt Damon and Robin Williams improvised a lot of their talk in the film "Good Will Hunting," which gave their exchanges greater sincerity and spontaneity. Some of the most memorable and poignant scenes in the movie were the improvised parts, such the "it is now not your fault" incident.

2. **Theatre**: Actors can improvise within the parameters of a scripted play to offer their performances more strength and spontaneity. In order to get sparkling perspectives and nuanced understandings of the characters and scenarios, administrators and writers every so often urge performers to improvise specific scenes or lines in the course of rehearsal.

3. **Television**: Comedies and improvisational comedy programs make tremendous use of improvisation of their performances. Actors improvise scenes, sketches, and games based on hints from the target market for comedic and impromptu moments in suggests like "Whose Line Is It Anyway?"

Conclusion

Adding improvisation to pre-written scenes can improve performances, boom realism, and inspire teamwork within the innovative method. In order to create dynamic and charming performances for a number of platforms, performers can without difficulty integrate scripted and improvised components with the aid of placing clean suggestions, staying targeted on dreams, and welcoming spontaneity. The use of improvisation in theatre, cinema, or tv complements performances via giving them greater intensity, spontaneity, and authenticity. The end result is memorable and effective moments that live with visitors lengthy after the curtain goes down or the credit roll.

9.Physicality and Voice

9.1 Exercises for voice projection and articulation

Whether you're presenting a presentation, performing on stage, or just having a chat, having good voice projection and articulation is crucial for efficient communication. These abilities provide you the ability to confidently and clearly communicate your message, ensuring that your audience pays attention and comprehends what you're saying. We'll go over a variety of exercises and methods in this tutorial to help you project and articulate your voice more clearly.

Voice Projection Exercises:

1. **Diaphragmatic Breathing**: The basis for projecting your voice is healthy breathing. Laying on your back, place a book on your abdomen to practice diaphragmatic breathing. Breathe deeply through your nose, feeling the book lift and your abdomen rise. Feel your belly drop as you gently release the breath through your mouth. By using this technique, you may effectively sustain your breath by using your diaphragm.

2. **Vocal Warm-Ups**: To prepare your voice, start your vocal practice sessions with warm-up activities. To start, softly engage your voice cords by humming or lip-trilling. As you warm up, gradually turn up the loudness and pitch range.

3. **Resonance Exercises**: To create a broader, richer sound, try out various resonating chambers in your body. Vocalize on a range of vowels and consonants to get comfortable with resonating in your mind, throat, and chest. Consider speaking into the rear of the space.

4. **Projection Drills**: Practice projecting your voice at various distances while standing in an open area. Speak softly at first, then progressively raise your level until you can be heard clearly across the room without straining your voice. Pay attention to sound uniformity and clarity.

5. **Articulation Exercises**: Effective communication requires clear articulation. Engage in tongue twisters and consonant-vowel blends to enhance your speaking clarity and diction. Keep an eye out for distinct vowel forms and sharp consonant sounds.

6. **Volume Control**: Practice dynamic range exercises to gain control over the volume of your voice. Whisper at first, then progressively raise your voice to a roar, then drop back to a whisper. This exercise assists you in maintaining effortless control over the intensity of your voice.

7. **Practice Voice Projection in Various Settings**: Get comfortable projecting your voice in a variety of settings, including a packed house, an outdoor plaza, and a sizable theatre. To retain clarity and resonance, modify your projection technique and volume to fit the acoustics of each location.

Articulation Exercises:

1. **Tongue Twisters**: These are a great way to work on your clarity and articulation. Practice sayings like "Peter Piper picked a peck of pickled peppers" or "She sells seashells by the seashore" gently at first, then progressively build up the pace without sacrificing intelligibility.

2. **Consonant Clusters**: Pay attention to pronouncing difficult consonant clusters like "thr," "spl," and "str." Repeat words that have these clusters, such "street," "splash," and "three," making sure to emphasize each consonant note.

3. **Vowel Modification**: To enhance resonance and clarity, try changing the vowel sounds. Make sure to precisely shape and elongate vowel sounds, steering clear of muted or nasal tones. Keep your jaw relaxed and your throat open.

4. **Sibilant Sounds**: Practice speaking clearly and firmly while pronouncing sibilant sounds like "s" and "sh". To practice hissing, hold these noises for a sustained period of time while breathing steadily and trying not to tense your mouth or tongue too much.

5. **Reading aloud**: Read aloud from a range of literature on a regular basis, such as speeches, prose, and poetry. As you read,

focus on your articulation, tempo, and intonation, trying to convey your words clearly and expressively.

6. **Mirror Exercises**: To evaluate your mouth form and facial motions, practice articulation exercises in front of a mirror. Pay attention to how each sound is pronounced and identify any spots where your face muscles are tense or rigid.

7. **Record and Review**: To assess your articulation and clarity, record yourself reading aloud or speaking, then play it back. Make a note of any places in your speech where you could be more exact or clear, and keep practicing those sounds.

With consistent practice, you can gradually enhance your vocal projection and articulation abilities by implementing these exercises. It takes time and effort to become proficient in these talents, so keep trying and being patient. You can have a confident, captivating speaking voice that grabs listeners' attention and connects with them if you practice consistently.

10. Actor Collaboration

10.1 The Actor's Place in a Production Team

An actor is a key player in the complex ecosystem of a production crew; they are the means by which the words and feelings of a script are translated into the stage or screen. They have to be more than just reciting lines; they have to be the character; they have to give it personality, complexity, and authenticity. Actors hold a special place within the larger framework of a production team, working together with directors, writers, producers, and other cast members to craft a seamless and captivating story experience. This essay will look at the many facets of the actor's job within the production crew, including their duties, difficulties, and contributions to the artistic process.

The interpretation and presentation of characters forms the core of an actor's job. Actors must delve deeply into the mind of their characters, whether they are playing historical figures, mythological creatures, or regular people, in order to fully comprehend their motives, desires, fears, and complexity. The process of bringing a part to life in a convincing and captivating way for an actor usually entails a great deal of character analysis, research, and rehearsal.

The capacity to communicate meaning and emotion through performance is essential to an actor's art. They have to be adept at using gesture, body language, facial expressions, and voice intonation to communicate to the audience the innermost feelings and ideas of their character. Actors give the script's words life by interpreting it in a way that gives it depth, resonance, and emotional truth.

Actors have to manage the dynamics of ensemble work in addition to their solo performances. They have to establish relationships with other cast members in order to foster chemistry, rapport, and cohesiveness on stage or screen. Building convincing relationships between characters and establishing a sense of authenticity and realism within the story depend on this collaborative aspect of acting.

Actors are integral members of the production team, offering their special talents, thoughts, and perspectives to the creative process even outside the boundaries of the stage or set. They work closely with directors, providing comments, suggestions, and interpretations to help meld the production's overall concept. Actors and directors collaborate to hone performances, develop character arcs, and guarantee coherence and continuity across the story through dialogue, experimentation, and discovery.

Additionally, actors work closely with writers, offering input on dialogue, character growth, and story dynamics to fortify the screenplay and heighten its dramatic effect. Their in-depth knowledge of motivation and character psychology can provide insightful analysis of the script's subtleties, enhancing the thematic resonance and giving characters more depth.

Actors are trusted by producers to give performances that connect with viewers—grabbing their interest, arousing empathy, and engrossing them in the narrative. Therefore, actors need to have a deep awareness of the dynamics, inclinations, and trends of the audience in order to customize their performances to entertain and engage audiences while maintaining the integrity of the character and the story.

Actors must also negotiate the practical difficulties and requirements of their profession during the course of the production, including scheduling, memorizing lines and blocking, taking care of their physical and mental health, and adjusting to the constantly shifting dynamics of the set. They need to be professional, resilient, and flexible enough to adjust to changing circumstances without losing sight of their art or original goal.

In conclusion, the actor plays a crucial and essential part in the production crew because they are the ones that bring the story to life and take the viewer to new places and experiences. In addition to their collaborative spirit, inventiveness, and dedication, which enhance the creative process and contribute to the overall success of the production, their ability to interpret, embody, and communicate the essence of their character is crucial for crafting a compelling and immersive narrative experience.

10.2 Collaborating with Directors, Co-Stars, and Support Personnel

In order to bring stories to life on stage and screen, performers collaborate closely with directors, co-stars, and support staff. Collaboration is at the core of both the filmmaking and theatrical processes. Since every member of the production team brings special skills and perspectives to the project, it takes a complex interplay of imagination, communication, and organization to pull this joint effort together. The dynamics of collaboration between performers, directors, co-stars, and support staff will be discussed in this essay, along with the roles, duties, and difficulties that arise when these parties come together to produce performances that are both memorable and captivating.

Working together with Directors: One of the most important collaborations in the creative process is that between directors and actors. The directors set the overall direction, tone, and style of the performance as well as the artistic direction of the production. In turn, directors provide direction, advice, and support to actors as they negotiate the subtleties of their roles and the story.

Open communication, respect for one another, and a shared dedication to the creative goal are necessary for performers and directors to work well together. In order to foster artistic risk-taking and originality, directors must establish a welcoming and inclusive environment where actors are open to guidance, experimentation, and exploration of new ideas.

Actors and directors have a collaborative discourse throughout rehearsal, delving into character motives, blocking, and performance decisions. Directors can provide performers with criticism on physicality, emotional tone, and line delivery, which can help them hone their performances and give their characters more nuance and authenticity.

Actors and directors continue to work together on the set beyond rehearsal, overcoming logistical obstacles to shoot or stage sequences while adhering to the creative vision of the play. While actors trust directors to provide them the direction and encouragement they need to give their greatest performances, directors depend on actors to translate their vision onto the screen or stage.

Collaborating with Co-Stars:

In order to create believable and captivating interactions on screen or stage, performers must develop chemistry, rapport, and trust with their co-stars. Acting is by its very nature a collaborative art form. In order to create engaging and genuine connections with viewers, actors—whether portraying rivals, friends, brothers, or romantic partners—must collaborate with one another.

Co-stars that work well together must have a mix of empathy, communication, and trust. To generate genuine and spontaneous moments in the performance, actors need to be intuitively aware of each other's emotions, cues, and rhythms.

Co-stars can experiment with numerous tactics and techniques during rehearsals to find the most interesting and effective way to depict their roles. This gives them the chance to explore the relationships, dynamics, and interactions of their characters. Actors can enhance their comprehension of the motivations and conflicts of their characters by participating in dialogue, role-playing, and improvisation activities.

Co-stars assist one another's performances on set or in the theatre by being alert and involved in the action to maintain the scene's coherence and consistency. They work closely together as well as with the director, modifying their performances as necessary to preserve the emotional authenticity of the characters' journey and the integrity of the story.

Collaborating with Support Personnel:

Along with directors and fellow performers, actors work closely with a variety of support staff members who are crucial to the success of a production. These experts, who range from makeup and costume designers to sound engineers and cinematographers, provide their skills and imagination to improve the performance's technical and aesthetic elements.

Support staff members help actors create realistic and engaging environments that help bring their characters and the story's world to life. They work together with costume designers to create outfits that accurately depict the motivations, histories, and personalities of their characters.

Together, they make sure that every little element enhances the production's overall look.

Makeup artists enable performers to fully inhabit their characters and communicate their inner thoughts and emotions by transforming their appearance through prosthetics, special effects, or subtle enhancements. Cinematographers and lighting specialists work in tandem with performers to document their performances on film, enhancing mood, atmosphere, and storytelling through the use of light, shadow, and composition.

Actors work in tandem with production staff to overcome technical obstacles, adjust to shifting circumstances, and guarantee that technical and visual components are seamlessly incorporated into performances. To create memorable and meaningful performances that engage with audiences, they must be able to interact amicably with all members of the production crew, solve problems creatively, and communicate effectively.

In conclusion, cooperation is essential to the theatrical and filmmaking processes, since actors collaborate closely with directors, co-stars, and crew members to bring stories to life on stage and screen. Actors and their colleagues use their combined talents and insights to create distinctive, captivating performances that captivate, inspire, and move audiences. They achieve this via open communication, mutual respect, and a shared dedication to the creative vision.

10.3 Recognizing and accommodating various directing philosophies.

Developing knowledge and flexibility in several different directing-schools of thought are vital for actors. Flexibility enables actors to adjust their method of acting and their means of collaborating to fit the vision and method of the director. Different directors bring different views, techniques, and skills to the table, influencing the overall spirit, tone, style, and state of production. Through knowing varying directing concepts, actors will learn to improve their functional, coherent, and innovative relationships with the director while benefiting themselves and the project.

The finer aspects of interpreting Directing Philosophies:

The spectrum of directing philosophies is so vast that they can be as traditional or innovative, naturalistic or stylized, and collaboratively driven or auteur-focused as the director intends. Therefore, a director's philosophy can be absolutely anything and is only limited by their frame of reference: the concepts and values given to them by the aforementioned teachers, immersion into the theories and drama of other artists, and personal interpretations. Some of directors may follow more traditional approach. For them, the primary aspects of the production are a good narrative, clear character development, and adherence to existing conventions in theatre. For this reason, these directors are often praised for their fidelity to their text. To them, every line must be delivered accurately, and every emotion intended by the author must be accurately displayed.

Others might take a more avant-garde or experimental stance, questioning accepted wisdom and stretching the bounds of form, structure, and style. These directors could place a high value on ambiguity, invention, and abstraction, pushing performers to experiment with unusual methods and interpretations in order to produce daring and provocative performances.

The level of collaboration that directors have with actors can also differ; they might be more hands-on and provide thorough advice and instruction, or they can be more laissez-faire and prioritize the actors' autonomy and creativity in creating their characters and performances.

Accommodating Different Directing Philosophies:

Actors must approach each collaboration with an open mind, a desire to adapt, and a commitment to supporting the director's vision while also bringing their own creative insights and instincts to the table in order to accommodate varying directing approaches.

Actors should concentrate on giving distinct, emotionally charged performances that strictly follow the script and the director's instructions when working with a traditional director. They should be open to criticism, guidance, and modifications as they work to both authentically and deeply convey the director's vision through their performance.

Actors should be willing to try out novel approaches, take chances with interpretations, and push the limits of their trade while working with filmmakers who have a more avant-garde or experimental style. Accepting ambiguity, abstraction, and uncertainty while maintaining an open mind to spontaneity and discovery during the creative process, they should have faith in the director's vision and direction.

Actors should take the lead in developing their roles and performances, contributing their own thoughts, viewpoints, and life experiences when directors value cooperation and actor autonomy. To improve their interpretation and the production's overall quality, they should have an open discussion with the director and provide comments, ideas, and insights.

performers and the director should have open channels of communication throughout the rehearsal process, with the performers asking for explanation, direction, and assistance as needed. They ought to take the initiative to voice any worries or inquiries they might have, standing up for their own artistic requirements while yet deferring to the director's authority and vision.

Handling Differences and Challenges: Taking into account various directing philosophies can enhance the creative process and produce unique and captivating outcomes, but it can also cause difficulties and confrontations for performers. Their instincts and creativity may be challenged by unclear expectations, differing artistic sensibilities, or competing directions.

Actors in these circumstances ought to handle difficulties with tact, professionalism, and patience, attempting to establish a common ground and encourage productive communication with the director. They should make an effort to keep a cooperative and solution-focused attitude, concentrating on coming up with original ideas to settle disagreements and realize the director's vision while simultaneously respecting their own artistic integrity and intuition.

Actors may have to rely on their own judgment and instincts to manage situations when tensions or disagreements continue. They must be willing to make concessions when needed while still standing up for their own artistic requirements and boundaries. The ultimate objective should be to develop a constructive working relationship with the director that is based on trust, respect, and a shared dedication to the project's success.

Conclusion:

Actors hoping to work well with directors and negotiate the intricacies of the creative process must understand and be able to work with a variety of directing philosophies. Actors may best serve the demands of the production by tailoring their performances and working methods to each director's distinct vision, style, and approach. This allows them to offer their own originality, insight, and enthusiasm to the project. Actors may improve their trade and broaden their artistic horizons in addition to helping the production succeed by being open with one another, being adaptable, and being dedicated to working together.

11. Ethics and Responsibility

11.1 Actors have an obligation to represent a range of viewpoints and cultures.

Through their roles in stage and film, actors are integral to the construction of cultural narratives and views. As a result, it is their duty to reflect in their work a wide variety of perspectives, cultures, and experiences. In the arts and in society at large, performers can promote greater understanding, empathy, and inclusion by taking on roles as individuals with varying histories, opinions, and identities. This essay will discuss the value of performers portraying a variety of perspectives and cultural backgrounds, the advantages and difficulties of doing so, and methods for advancing diversity and inclusiveness in acting.

Importance of Representation:

To guarantee that a range of perspectives and experiences are acknowledged and embraced, representation in the arts is crucial. Through their performances, performers can help audiences become more conscious, empathetic, and understanding by challenging stereotypes, dismantling prejudices, and amplifying marginalized voices.

Actors have the ability to validate the identities and experiences of audiences by taking on characters from a variety of backgrounds and cultures. This broadens the perspectives of individuals who might not be as familiar with different cultures and points of view.

Cultural Authenticity and Sensitivity:

Actors must approach their roles with authenticity, empathy, and respect when portraying many cultures and identities. This entails carrying out in-depth study, getting feedback from community people or cultural consultants, and having discussions with colleagues to make sure that their representation is accurate, nuanced, and devoid of damaging preconceptions or misunderstandings.

In addition to appreciating the subtleties and complexity of identity and experience, actors should make an effort to comprehend the historical, social, and cultural circumstances in which their characters live. They should be aware of their own prejudices and presumptions and keep an open mind to criticism and comments from the people whose viewpoints they wish to represent.

Benefits of Diversity in Acting:

Accepting variety in acting enhances the artistic environment and advances social justice and equity by encouraging originality, creativity, and authenticity in narrative. Actors enhance the vibrancy and dynamic portrayal of the human experience by incorporating their own distinct opinions, experiences, and cultural backgrounds into their performances.

Diverse casting gives actors from all backgrounds the chance to show off their skills and add to the richness and diversity of the arts by increasing the representation and visibility of marginalized communities. It also contributes to the questioning of conventional ideas of genius, beauty, and deservingness, making room for a greater variety of voices and narratives to be acknowledged.

Challenges and Considerations:

While there are numerous advantages to portraying a variety of perspectives and cultural backgrounds in acting, actors must also overcome certain obstacles and take certain factors into account. Gatekeepers in the industry who are hesitant to invest in diverse storytelling or who are averse to change may push back against them.

Actors may also struggle with issues of representation, authenticity, and appropriation, especially when taking on roles that are different from their own in terms of identity or heritage. Actors should approach these roles with humility, understanding, and a willingness to learn because their portrayal could influence how viewers view and comprehend various identities and cultures.

Strategies for Promoting Diversity and Inclusion:

Ways to Encourage Diversity and Inclusion in performing: Actors, casting directors, producers, directors, and other industry stakeholders must work together to promote diversity and inclusion in the performing profession. By promoting diverse productions, elevating the voices of underrepresented groups, and speaking out against discriminatory practices, actors may promote better representation and opportunities for underrepresented communities on and off screen.

It is the duty of casting directors and producers to cast in a genuine and inclusive manner, to look for talent from a variety of backgrounds, and to make sure that the choices they make reflect the diversity of the world in which we live. Employing diverse creative teams—including writers, directors, and designers—who each offer their own special insights and life experiences to the storytelling process can also be a top priority.

Stakeholders in the industry can encourage diversity and inclusivity in acting by funding projects and programs that give underrepresented actors access to opportunities and mentorship, as well as tools and training to assist them advance in their careers. Additionally, they can speak out against institutionalized prejudices and hurdles in the field and support laws and procedures that promote greater fairness and representation for all.

Conclusion:

In order to foster greater understanding, empathy, and inclusiveness in the arts and society at large, actors have a commitment to reflect a variety of perspectives and cultures in their performance. Through their performances, actors can promote a more vibrant and inclusive artistic landscape where all voices are acknowledged, supported, and cherished by embracing diversity, honesty, and sensitivity. Actors may contribute to the creation of a world in which everyone's story has the chance to be heard and valued by working together, advocating for social justice, and maintaining a strong sense of social justice.

11.2 Ethical issues in depicting delicate or contentious characters or subjects.

Actors, directors, writers, and producers face a variety of ethical dilemmas while portraying sensitive or divisive characters or subjects in theatre, cinema, television, and other media. A dedication to integrity and social responsibility, thoughtful analysis, empathy, and a commitment to authenticity and representation are all necessary while navigating the ethical challenges of storytelling. Other considerations include injury, exploitation, and cultural appropriation. This essay will examine the moral dilemmas that arise when portraying sensitive or divisive personalities or subjects, the obligations placed on artists and performers, and methods for handling these difficulties with tact and honesty.

Authenticity and Representation:

The necessity of authenticity and accurate representation is one of the main ethical considerations when illustrating sensitive or controversial individuals or subjects. Whether they are tackling contentious social problems, depicting characters from underrepresented groups, or delving into delicate subjects like trauma or mental illness, producers must make an effort to represent these experiences with complexity, empathy, and respect.

Conducting in-depth research, getting feedback from others who have lived the experience, and approaching the topic with humility and an open mind are all necessary for authentic depiction. It is imperative for creators to put authenticity ahead of sensationalism or exploitation, with the goal of capturing the nuance and complexity of the human experience in all its diversity.

Harm and Exploitation:

The possibility of harm and exploitation is another ethical consideration when portraying sensitive or controversial persons or issues. Without taking into account the effects on performers, viewers, or those who have experienced the tragedy first hand, depicting traumatic or contentious material might reinforce negative stereotypes, cause emotional pain, or fuel discrimination and stigma.

It is the duty of creators to handle delicate subject matter with care and attention, taking precautions to lessen any possible harm and making sure that their work is presented in an ethical and responsible way. This could entail supplying trigger warnings, presenting sources of assistance or more details, or speaking with subject-matter specialists to guarantee that the material is presented truthfully and delicately.

Cultural Appropriation:

Another moral dilemma that comes up when portraying characters or subjects from other people's cultures or groups is cultural appropriation. When individuals of a dominant culture exploit aspects of a marginalized culture without properly appreciating, respecting, or recognizing their value, this is known as appropriation.

When working on culturally sensitive material, actors, writers, directors, and producers need to be aware of the power dynamics at play and try to avoid repeating negative narratives or stereotypes. This could entail asking permission or cooperation from people who have lived the experience, conferring with cultural experts or community members, and treating the topic with dignity and humility.

Informed Consent and Agency:

The question of informed consent and agency comes up in the context of performance as another ethical dilemma. Performers who play sensitive or controversial roles might have to work on emotionally or mentally taxing or demanding material, which could be detrimental to their mental and physical health.

Directors, producers, and casting agencies must put actors' welfare and agency first, making sure they are completely aware of the role's requirements and any potential difficulties.

In addition to being given the option to accept or reject parts that can be emotionally taxing or detrimental to their health, actors should also be given the assistance and tools they need to handle the demands of the stage.

Strategies for Ethical Storytelling:

Telling a story with care and intention is necessary to negotiate the moral challenges of presenting sensitive or divisive people or topics. In order to make sure that their work is moral, responsible, and considerate of other viewpoints and experiences, creators might employ a number of tactics:

1. **Perform in-depth study**: Before depicting delicate subject matter, authors should carry out in-depth research to get a deeper comprehension of the relevant concerns, such as the cultural relevance, historical background, and the experiences of those impacted by the subject matter.

2. **Consult experts and those who have lived the experience**: Experts, cultural consultants, and people who have lived the experience can offer insightful opinions and viewpoints that help guide the representation of sensitive or divisive characters or issues.

3. **Put authenticity and representation first**: Writers should make an effort to represent characters and themes in an authentic manner, empathetically, respectfully, and with integrity,

expressing the subtleties and complexity of the human experience.

4. **Provide resources and support**: When dealing with sensitive subject matter, authors should include options for additional information or support, such as helplines, trigger warnings, or groups that aid people impacted by the concerns depicted.

5. **Encourage cooperation and inclusivity**: Working together with people who have different experiences and backgrounds may make sure that the narrative process is courteous, inclusive, and represents a variety of viewpoints and views.

6. **Pay attention to criticism and respond to it**: Artists should be receptive to criticism and comments from the public as well as from critics. They should also be prepared to address any issues or concerns brought up regarding the moral implications of their work.

Conclusion:

The ethical ramifications of portraying sensitive or controversial persons or issues in the media must be carefully considered. It is the duty of creators to handle delicate subject matter with sincerity, compassion, and morality, giving actors' and viewers' autonomy and well-being equal weight. Artists have the ability to promote greater understanding, empathy, and inclusivity in the arts and society at large by using a deliberate and considered approach to storytelling.

11.3 Juggling creative liberty with social

Actors must walk a fine line between social responsibility and artistic freedom when practicing their trade, especially when taking on roles that deal with touchy or divisive issues. Actors have the opportunity to fully inhabit their roles and delve into the depths of human experience, but social responsibility demands that they think about how their portrayals could affect audiences, local communities, and society as a whole. This essay will examine the conflict between acting with creative liberty and acting with social duty, the ethical issues raised, and methods for achieving a balance between the two.

Creative Liberty in Acting:

A key component of acting is creative liberty, which gives actors the freedom to fully embrace their roles and give them life, subtlety, and authenticity. It includes the liberty to explore the emotional, psychological, and physical aspects of their characters as well as to produce original interpretations of the script.

In order to fully realize their artistic potential, push limits, and provide performances that really connect with audiences, actors need to have the freedom to express themselves freely. It allows artists to give their characters life and give them nuance, humanity, and complexity by drawing on their imagination, intuition, and personal experiences.

Social Responsibility in Acting:

The foundation of the acting profession is creative independence, but it must be balanced with social responsibility, especially when performing roles that deal with delicate or divisive matters. Actors have a voice and a platform that can change social attitudes and behaviours, societal narratives, and public debate. This impact carries with it an obligation to think about the larger social ramifications of their work and to make sure that their representation is morally sound, courteous, and sensitive to cultural differences.

Actors have a social obligation to consider how their portrayal may affect audiences, local communities, and society as a whole. Actors must commit to honesty and integrity, as well as approach their roles with humility and empathy. It also requires understanding how structural injustices, power relationships, and cultural sensitivities may influence how particular individuals or issues are portrayed.

Balancing Creative Liberty and Social Responsibility:

In acting, striking a balance between social duty and creative license necessitates a sophisticated approach that considers the project's unique setting, substance, and audience. Actors have to think about the wider social and cultural relevance of the subject matter, the possible good or harm to oppressed populations, and the ethical ramifications of how they depict the material.

Interacting freely and cooperatively with directors, writers, and other cast members is one way to strike a balance between artistic freedom and social responsibility. Actors can collaborate to address ethical issues, explore the subtleties of their roles, and make sure their portrayals are truthful and respectful by creating a welcoming and inclusive creative atmosphere.

An alternative strategy is to carry out in-depth study and ask people with first-hand knowledge or subject-matter expertise for their opinions. Speaking with advocates, community leaders, or cultural advisers can offer insightful opinions and useful information that can help with how sensitive or divisive personalities or issues are portrayed.

Actors can also push for more social justice, diversity, and inclusivity in the entertainment business by using their platform. Actors have the potential to positively impact social change and foster a deeper sense of understanding and empathy in society by endorsing projects that stress honest depiction, challenge stereotypes, and elevate underrepresented perspectives.

Conclusion:

One of the biggest challenges facing performers today is striking a balance between social duty and artistic liberty. This means navigating the intricate web of storytelling with empathy, sensitivity, and honesty. Actors have the liberty to fully delve into their characters' depths and produce captivating performances, but they also have a social responsibility to think about the wider social and cultural ramifications of their work and to make sure that their representation is inclusive, ethical, and respectful. Actors can use their craft to further knowledge, empathy, and constructive social change by finding a balance between social consciousness and creative expression.

12. Artistic Reflection

Stage of Souls: A Journey Through the Actor's Life

In the limelight's glow, the actor stands tall,
A chameleon of emotions, heeding every call.
From stage to screen, he weaves his art,
A masterful performance, a work of heart.

With each role embraced, a new life he'll wear,
Inhabiting characters with depth and flair.
From tragedy to comedy, he'll effortlessly glide,
Captivating audiences far and wide.

But behind the curtain, the actor's soul hides,
A labyrinth of dreams, fears, and strides.
For fame's allure can be a double-edged sword,
Bringing adoration, yet leaving hearts ignored.

Through highs and lows, the actor will tread,
Seeking truth in scripts, in words unsaid.
For in this grand theatre of life's grand stage,
He finds his essence, his passion, his sage.

So, here's to the actor, whose life's a play,
Navigating through the scencs, day by day.
For in every role, he finds a piece of truth,
An eternal quest for beauty, in age and youth.

13. TRIBUTE TO THE FATHER OF INDIAN CINEMA THE GREAT DADASAHEB PHALKE

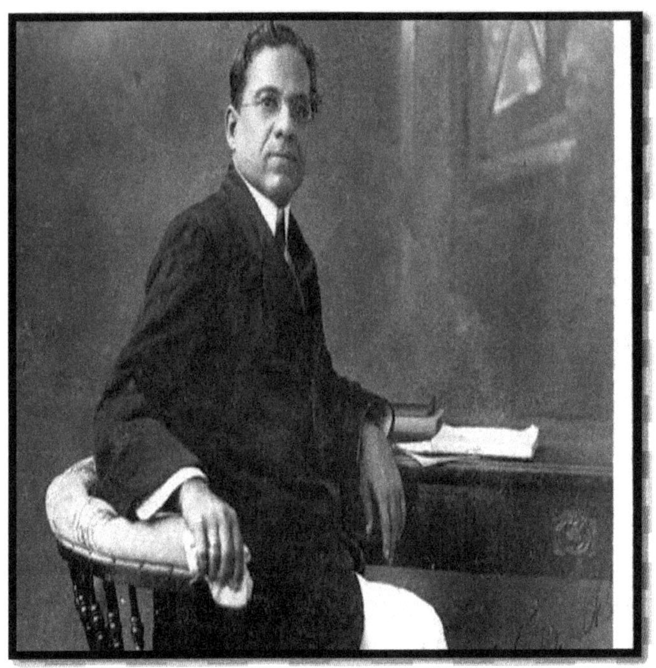

When paying tribute to Dadasaheb Phalke, it is impossible to avoid being overwhelmed by the enormous legacy he left behind—a mark that is permanently inscribed into the very fabric of Indian film. I am drawn to Phalke's significant influence on the development of Indian cinema and the entertainment industry as a whole since I am an author and a lover of acting.

Often referred to as the "father of Indian cinema," Dadasaheb Phalke was a visionary whose love of storytelling had no bounds. Dadasaheb Phalke dared to dream large in an era when moving pictures were still a novel concept. Armed only with limitless creativity and an unyielding resolve to realize his goal, he set off on a challenging adventure.

The year 1913 saw the premiere of Phalke's masterwork, "Raja Harishchandra," which marked the beginning of Indian movie history. Against all difficulties and with little funding, Phalke created an enduring story that enthralled viewers and established the groundwork for a thriving business. His innovative approach and unwavering perseverance cleared the path for other actors and directors to come.

However, Dadasaheb Phalke's accomplishments go much beyond the world of cinema. He was a maverick and a trailblazer who dared to question the current quo and push the bounds of what was conceivable. His ground-breaking methods and inventive storytelling style transformed the film industry, making a lasting impression on a worldwide scale.

As a writer, Phalke's unflinching dedication to his work and unrelenting quest of perfection motivate me. He was more than just a director; he was a storyteller in the best sense of the word, crafting tales that connected with viewers of all ages. His movies explored themes of love, sacrifice, and the triumph of the human spirit, offering viewers a deeper look into the human condition than just light entertainment.

We celebrate a legacy that continues to influence the fundamental fabric of Indian film by paying respect to Dadasaheb Phalke, not just a man. His contributions have endured, which is proof of the storytelling medium's enduring strength. As actors, it is our responsibility to uphold the creative and innovative mantle that he so bravely accepted. We are the bearers of his heritage.

In "Leela," I try to convey the essence of Phalke's talent, honouring a man whose vision went above the limitations of his time. We are inspired to dream large, to overcome obstacles, and to never lose sight of the transformational potential of art by his incredible path. Even though Dadasaheb Phalke is no longer with us, his influence can still be seen in every Indian film, serving as a beacon of hope for future generations.

14. Inspiration from the Greats
Examples of Best Actors with Their Bio

DEV ANAND

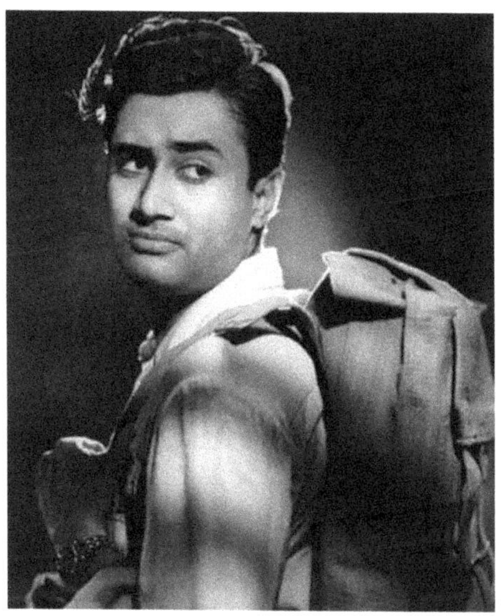

Known as the "Evergreen Hero" of Indian cinema, Dev Anand was a renowned actor whose charm, sense of style, and love of telling stories made him a memorable character in the history of the Indian film industry. Dev Anand was born in Shakar Garh, British India, on September 26, 1923. His remarkable rise from struggling newbie to cinematic superstar is a tribute to his brilliance, tenacity, and unshakable dedication to his profession. Shakar Garh is now in Pakistan.

The essence of Dev Anand's lasting influence is his unique charisma and captivating on-screen persona. He enthralled audiences with his effortless charm and elegant demeanour, complete with his signature tilted hat, puff of hair, and contagious smile. Dev Anand was a constant favourite with audiences of all ages because he radiated a young energy and vitality, whether he was romancing leading ladies on screen or playing the archetypal urban sophisticate.

Dev Anand's ability to play characters with nuance, complexity, and emotional resonance was one of his best acting qualities. From the melancholic anti-hero in "Guide" to the endearing outlaw in "Hare Rama Hare Krishna," he possessed a talent for convincingly and authentically bringing to life imperfect but likable characters. His genuine acting approach and subtle grace distinguished him from other actors of his day in his performances.

Beyond just his acting abilities, Dev Anand has made significant contributions to Indian cinema as a ground-breaking filmmaker and imaginative storyteller. He was a key figure in determining the direction of Indian cinema as the founder of Navketan Films, bringing cutting-edge methods and narrative motifs that completely changed the business. Movies such as "Baazi," "Guide," and "Jewel Thief" demonstrated not just his acting prowess but also his vision as a filmmaker and creative brilliance.

Dev Anand's films were distinguished by their universal themes and ageless appeal. His films connected with viewers of all ages, cutting across linguistic and cultural barriers, whether they were probing the moral difficulties of society or the intricacies of love and relationships. He had a lasting impression on Indian film with his cinematic narrative, which aimed to inspire, amuse, and prompt thinking.

Apart from his triumph on screen, Dev Anand was renowned for his progressive principles and dedication to societal transformation. Fans and colleagues alike respected and admired him for using his platform as a public person and filmmaker to advocate for causes like social justice, secularism, and freedom of expression. For millions of others, he served as an inspiration and source of hope because of his unyielding adherence to his beliefs and his courageous search for the truth.

Dev Anand received multiple honours and recognitions for his enormous contributions to Indian cinema, including the Dadasaheb Phalke Award, the highest honour in Indian cinema, and the Padma Bhushan, India's third-highest civilian award. Actors and filmmakers in India and other countries continue to draw inspiration from his legacy, which has had an immense impact on the business.

In conclusion, the extraordinary career of Dev Anand is a brilliant illustration of the transformational potential of acting and narrative. He has cemented his place as an absolute legend of Indian cinema with his ability to amuse, provoke, and inspire through his performances and films. His enduring contributions have not only delighted audiences but also advanced the field of cinema to unprecedented levels, creating a legacy that will last for many years to come.

DILIP KUMAR

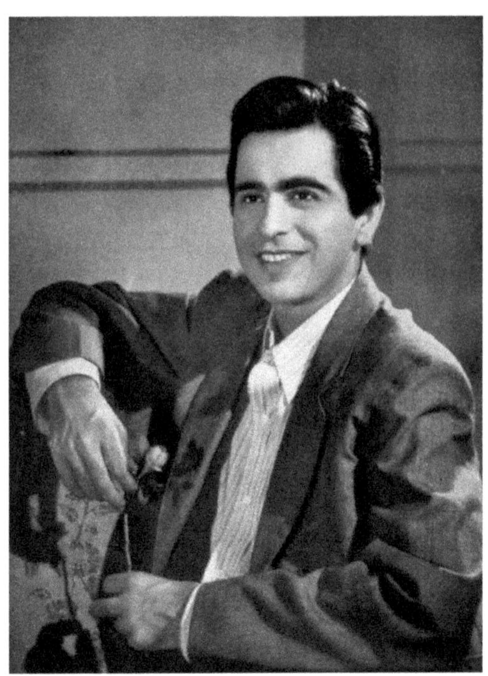

Dilip Kumar is a model actor whose contributions to acting transcend boundaries and generations. He is frequently considered as one of the best performers in Indian cinema history. Upon entering the film industry, Muhammad Yusuf Khan, who was born on December 11, 1922, in Peshawar, Pakistan, went by the screen name Dilip Kumar. His more than six-decade career has had a profound impact on Indian cinema and influenced a great number of performers and directors around the world.

Dilip Kumar's amazing versatility and ability to inhabit numerous characters with honesty and depth are at the core of his enduring legacy. His portrayals were distinguished by their subtle comprehension of human emotions and remarkable aptitude at expressing them on screen. Whether playing the troubled prince in "Mughal-e-Azam" or the angst-ridden lover in "Devdas," Dilip Kumar embodied a unique sensitivity and passion to his parts that struck a profound chord with viewers.

Dilip Kumar's ability to convey nuance and understatement was one of his most distinctive acting qualities. He possessed a special talent for subtly expressing a wide range of emotions through movements and facial expressions, frequently without the use of overt theatrics or dramatic speech. His performances had a sense of reality and emotional depth that distinguished him from his peers thanks to this subtle technique.

In the movie "Ganga Jamuna," which demonstrated his versatility as an actor, Dilip Kumar gave an outstanding performance as the lead character, Jamuna. He received a lot of praise for his depiction of a straightforward villager stuck between obligations to his family and moral quandaries, which cemented his status as a formidable performer. The box office triumph of the movie strengthened his reputation as the "Tragedy King" of Indian cinema.

In addition to his skill as a serious actor, Dilip Kumar was also a great comedy actor and charming light-hearted character. His ease with which he switched from serious dramas and light-hearted romances in movies like "Andaz" and "Azaad" demonstrated his breadth and adaptability as an actor.

Dilip Kumar was renowned for his acting abilities as well as his dedication to his work and collaborative nature. Alongside actress Vyjayanthimala, he had a storied on-screen relationship that spanned multiple classic films, such as "Naya Daur" and "Madhumati." Their on-screen chemistry was evident, and their scenes together are regarded as some of the most memorable in Indian film history.

Dilip Kumar became a cultural icon and an inspiration to upcoming performers and filmmakers, so his impact went beyond the big screen. He won over both audiences and co-workers with his commitment to his art, humility, and sincerity. He was a paragon of professionalism and creative brilliance in addition to being a gifted performer.

Dilip Kumar received a great deal of praise for his work in Indian cinema, including the Dadasaheb Phalke Award, the highest honour in Indian cinema, and the Padma Bhushan, India's third-highest civilian award. His influence on the business is immense, and future generations of performers are still motivated to achieve greatness by his example.

To sum up, Dilip Kumar's remarkable career is a brilliant illustration of the transformational potential of acting. His portrayal of characters endowed with emotional resonance, realism, and depth distinguished him as a genuine cinematic legend. He raised the bar for acting as a profession while simultaneously providing viewers with everlasting entertainment.

AMITABH BACHCHAN

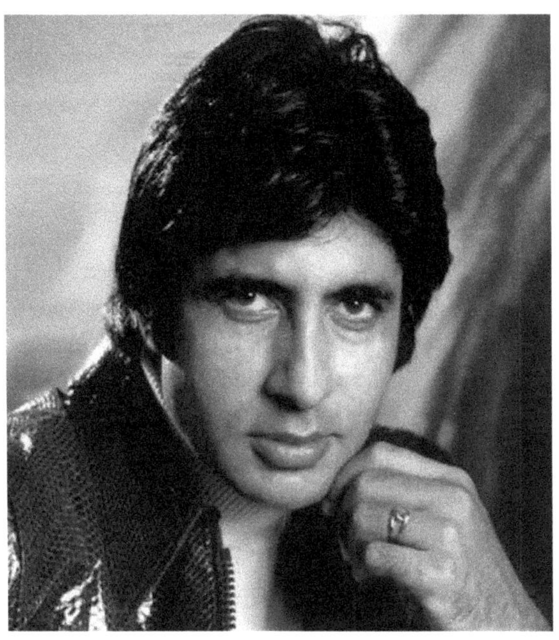

The iconic actor of Indian cinema, Amitabh Bachchan, personifies acting as a transforming art form. Born in Allahabad, India, on October 11, 1942, Bachchan's transformation from a struggling upstart to a renowned icon is evidence of his unmatched brilliance, tenacity, and commitment to his trade. Over the course of a five-decade career, Bachchan has irrevocably changed the Indian cinema business and continues to serve as an inspiration to a new generation of actors everywhere.

Bachchan's captivating on-screen persona and charismatic demeanour are fundamental to his lasting influence. At six feet two inches tall, he had a massive build that went well with his larger-than-life on-screen character. Whether he was playing the irate young man opposing social injustice in "Zanjeer" and "Deewaar" or the loving father figure in "Baghban" and "Piku," Bachchan brought a sense of gravity and intensity to his roles that enthralled viewers of all ages.

Being able to play a variety of roles with unmatched authenticity and conviction is one of Bachchan's most distinctive acting qualities. He demonstrated his variety and ability as an actor by skilfully navigating the gamut of human emotions, from intense dramas to light-hearted comedy. His distinctive baritone voice and flawless diction added to his on-screen demeanour, giving his performances a weight and authority.

Bachchan had many difficulties and disappointments in his path to become a household name. He encountered rejection early in his career and had difficulty establishing himself in the film business. But in the end, his tenacity and unyielding resolve paid off when he was cast in major motion pictures like "Anand" and "Zanjeer," which shot him to stardom and made him the current biggest celebrity in Indian cinema.

Bachchan's portrayal of the "angry young man" image, which struck a deep chord with viewers during the socio-political unrest of the 1970s, is one of his most enduring contributions to Indian cinema. In addition to showcasing his acting talent, movies like "Deewaar" and "Sholay" captured the hopes and frustrations of a generation dealing with structural injustice and inequity.

Bachchan's remarkable career is distinguished not just by his memorable performances but also by his daring to try new things and push the bounds of traditional narrative. Whether working with avant-garde directors like Yash Chopra and Ramesh Sippy or taking on unusual parts in movies like "Black" and "Paa," he continually changed himself, demonstrating his capacity to change and expand as an actor.

In addition to his contributions to film, Bachchan has influenced many other areas of Indian life and culture. In addition to being a highly regarded actor, he is also regarded as a social influencer, philanthropist, and cultural hero. He is regarded as a role model for millions of people worldwide due to his elegant manner, humility, and eloquence, which have won him the respect and affection of both colleagues and admirers.

Bachchan has received a great deal of acclaim for his enormous contributions to Indian cinema, including multiple National Film Awards and the Padma Vibhushan, which is India's second-highest civilian honour. IIe has had an enormous impact on the business, and his legacy motivates a new generation of actors to strive for excellence.

Finally, Amitabh Bachchan's unmatched career is a brilliant illustration of the transformational potential of acting. Being able to portray people with nuance, realism, and emotional resonance has cemented his place as an absolute icon in Indian cinema. He has created a legacy that will last for many years by entertaining audiences and pushing the boundaries of acting with his classic performances.

DADA KONDKE

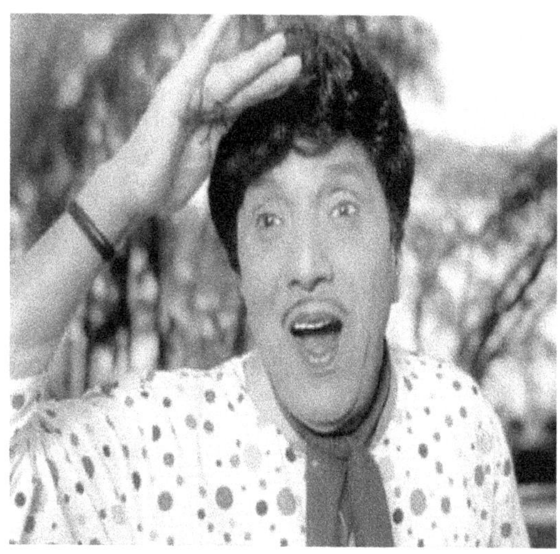

Known affectionately as the "King of Comedy" in Marathi cinema, Dada Kondke was a legendary actor who won over audiences all over Maharashtra, India, with his distinct sense of humour and unabashed storytelling. Kondke was born on August 8, 1932, in a small Maharashtra town. His extraordinary journey from modest beginnings to become one of the most recognizable characters in Marathi film is a credit to his brilliance, tenacity, and unmatched sense of humour.

Dada Kondke's unparalleled ability to captivate audiences with his boisterous performances and sharp banter is the foundation of his enduring legacy. With a great sense of observation and a razor-sharp wit, he was able to portray characters that the average person could relate to. He frequently used comedy and irreverence to represent the hardships and quirks of daily life.

Kondke's remarkable ability to bring comedy and brightness to even the most routine settings were one of his most distinctive acting qualities. He had a special gift for discovering humour in the everyday and turning ordinary situations into hilarious gems, whether he was playing the charming outlaw in "Pandu Hawaldar" or the foolish everyman in "Songadya." Audiences of all ages adored him for his double entendre expertise, slapstick antics, and perfect timing.

Beyond just his acting abilities, Kondke has made significant contributions to Marathi cinema as a trailblazing writer and filmmaker. He not only acted in several of his own films, but he also wrote and directed them, bringing his own comic sensibilities to every facet of the production. In addition to showcasing his acting prowess, movies like "Pandu Havaldar," "Sasarche Dhotar," and "Songadya" solidified his reputation as a cultural hero and a major contributor to the revival of Marathi cinema.

Kondke's films were distinguished by their unreserved acceptance of social satire and commentary. He tackled important societal topics including gender inequality, corruption, and class divisions through his hilarious stories and vibrant characters, frequently employing satire as a means of thought-provoking and conversation-starting. Kondke's films were humorous and light-hearted even though they dealt with serious issues; this allowed them to be watched by a broad audience and still convey important ideas.

Dada Kondke was well-known for his charity and altruism off-screen in addition to his accomplishments on screen. He used his celebrity and power to improve society by getting involved in a number of humanitarian endeavours and social concerns. He gained respect and adoration both on and off the screen because of his humility, compassion, and dedication to his roots, which won him over both fans and colleagues.

Dada Kondke received many honours and prizes, including the Maharashtra State Film Award for Best Actor and the Maharashtra State Film Award for Best Director, in appreciation of his enormous contributions to Marathi cinema. Actors and filmmakers in Maharashtra and beyond continue to draw inspiration from his legacy, which has had an immense impact on the industry.

To sum up, Dada Kondke's extraordinary career is a brilliant illustration of the transformational potential of humour and narrative. His reputation as a genuine giant of Marathi cinema has been cemented by his ability to amuse, provoke, and inspire audiences through his performances and films. He has left a legacy that will last for many decades by his timeless contributions, which have not only delighted audiences but also advanced the comedy genre to new heights.

Let's pause as we approach the last chapter of this engrossing voyage into the realm of acting to consider the wonder that occurs when expression and imagination come together. An actor's life is a tapestry of passion, devotion, and unwavering pursuit of excellence, from the heart-pounding auditions to the electrifying opening night. May the inspiration spark within you ignite as you turn the pages of this book, pushing you to step bravely into the spotlight. Because every script has a universe just waiting to be realized, and every actor is a storyteller waiting to have their voice heard.

Thus, keep in mind that the stage is your canvas and your performance is a work of art in the making while you explore the vast world of performing arts. Allow your imagination to reach new heights, enjoy the excitement of creativity, and embrace the thrill of the unknown. You have the ability to take viewers to places beyond their wildest expectations with every part you play and every character you bring to life.

May you face every situation with bravery, every obstacle with perseverance, and every failure as a chance for improvement. May you find happiness in pursuing your craft, contentment in pursuing your ambitions, and success in pursuing your authentic self as you navigate the ups and downs of this incredible path. Cheers to those who dare to follow their passions with unflinching determination—dreamers, believers, and daring spirits. Go forth and shine, for the world is yours to seize. The stage is set and the spotlight is waiting for you.

अयं संसारः एकः मञ्चः अस्ति तथा च वयं सर्वे भिन्नाः भिन्नाः चरित्रभूमिकाः निर्वहन्तः स्मः

www.ingramcontent.com/pod-product-compliance
Lightning Source LLC
LaVergne TN
LVHW051101180726

843512LV00020B/1561